THE
THREE RECTORIES

THE
THREE RECTORIES

WITHINGTON – KENNINGTON – LITTLE GADDESDEN

Constance Lane

2004

Published by
PHILLIMORE & CO. LTD
Shopwyke Manor Barn, Chichester, West Sussex, England

© Barbara Cassell, 2004

ISBN 1 86077 296 X

Printed and bound in Great Britain by
THE CROMWELL PRESS
Trowbridge, Wiltshire

Contents

FOREWORD

by

Barbara Cassell (née Lane)

This account of life in the 'Three Rectories' was written by my aunt Constance Lane (always known as 'Cooie'). She was a gifted and entertaining person: she could sing well, had had some poems published, and wrote this book at the end of her life, but I suppose she would have thought of herself as an artist.

One gets glimpses of her life from the book. She never married though she had various admirers; perhaps 'Mr Right' was killed in the 1914 war; perhaps nobody actually asked her because her health was not good; or her lack of punctuality worried them. I know that many male friends were very distressed at her death in 1944. Although aged only 20 at this time, I was dealing with her affairs as my father (her brother) was working abroad and could not get to England.

She certainly had an interesting life: she was a contemporary of Edith Sitwell, and my grandmother was required to 'bring out' Cooie and Edith together – not a great success with Edith, as she hated every minute of it – though she and Cooie were good friends at the time.

Enough money was found to acquire a long lease of a house in Paultons Square, Chelsea (not so grand in those days) and Cooie had this house until her death. She let the top half of the house, had a housekeeper, and did quite a lot of painting herself. She also had a studio at my grandmother's house. So she was able to go on visits to various relations, including to Italy to stay with Edith Sitwell's parents at Montegufoni, where Sir George had made a second famous garden. Cooie helped to immortalise this garden by painting it. She was invited to stay to help keep Lady Ida away from gambling! And to paint.

Cooie had attended the Slade School of Art and among her tutors were Tonks and Orpen. She made friends with Dora Carrington and between them they painted three frescoes at Ashridge House (now Ashridge Management College), which are still there. The commission would have come via Lady Brownlow, who was a cousin of my grandmother (Cooie's mother). She made several lifelong friends, amongst whom were Sir William Nicholson and his wife Winifred, and their son Ben used to visit her at Paultons Square. Sir William sketched Cooie.

Her life was fairly happy, though she obviously lacked her own family and normal home. My grandmother died in 1936 and because of this the family home at Nettleden House was sold, so Cooie took the lease of a cottage at St Margaret's. My father was a Colonial Service judge by this time and so was abroad. My brother and I spent some of our school holidays with her and so, of course, she became an important person to us.

I feel that this small book is of interest today perhaps because life is now so different.

INTRODUCTION

In writing about the parsonages where my parents were brought up, and the one at Little Gaddesden in which I was born, I want to show the changes in dress, education, in moral and religious outlook, and in taste, which strike me as I look through the old letters and diaries, and yet stress the essential sameness of human nature. These three rectories represent the mixture of aristocracy and the middle class, once characteristics of so many households in England.

The rectories, standing in a middle position in the English world, between the rich and the poor, the learned and the ignorant, the dedicated and the pleasure-loving, taught their children to make the best of things, and, looking to a higher good, to deal with life as it came to them. Is it fanciful to think this described by another of my mother's sayings, 'Le mieux est l'ennemi du bien', with its note of wisdom and irony, as it to ask, what can be better than 'le bien'? Is not 'le mieux' the region of restless endeavour, the attempt to better oneself, to improve the world? Is not 'le bien' the state of active repose of the mystics, the happy mean of the Greeks?

The old letters and diaries call up pleasant pictures of women in their crinolines, and their bunched up dresses; of the sporting events, the men with top hats, cravats, and canes. But how dreadful for a girl with consumption to go to balls in silks and satins as my aunt Emma did!

And I wonder what kind of boots and gaiters grandpapa wore to go out shooting, and of what pattern was his gun. And in London, how did the Lanes of Kennington Parsonage get about? It seems 'people like us' did not keep a carriage, in spite of the stable and stable yard of which St Mark's Vicarage boasted. No, they took a horse bus or, I suppose, hired a cab on special occasions.

I myself regret the passing of the horses that then shared everyone's lives. Each had a name, whether a hunter or a cab horse, and each a character of his or her own. I like to fancy that the idiosyncrasies of their owners were in a way influenced by the ways of the horses. Foresight and understanding are needed to get the best out of a horse; you cannot 'start up' without a flick of the whip, or a word, or at least a touch of the reins. Besides, your horse has to be harnessed, and each has his own way of starting. Thrift and planning of all kinds were then much vaunted, and the horses had to be considered. The various equipages they drew were an integral part of the Victorian picture – whether phaeton, barouche, basket, spider, dog cart or bus ...

My book, then, is a series of pictures – of people, of horses, of places, little prints, views and souvenirs – or shall I call it a counterpoint, with many themes winding into one another, of varied strains, the echoes of dead voices, the scratching of old pens, the rumbling of long-ago carriages, the sound of trotting hoofs and catches of forgotten songs?

One

WITHINGTON RECTORY

The family, of which my mother's father was the fifth, consisted of nine brothers and two sisters. They were the children of Charles, 2nd Lord Talbot, who was Viceroy of Ireland from 1817 to 1820, and Frances Thomasine Lambart of Beau Park, County Meath.

The eldest son Charles, Viscount Ingestre, was drowned in the Danube at the age of 24. Henry, the second, a sailor, lived to become 18th Earl of Shrewsbury. At 24 he was captain of a frigate, in which he fought in the last battle under sail, at Navarino. The fourth son, John, was Attorney-General to the Prince of Wales and Recorder of Windsor; while George Gustavus, my grandfather, took holy orders, and became Rector of Withington in Gloucestershire. Gilbert, the seventh son, became Monsignor Talbot, a canon of Rome; and the eighth son, Wellington Patrick (called Wellington because the Duke was his godfather), was a captain in the army and Sergeant at Arms to the House of Lords. Gerald, the youngest, was born in 1817; tradition says he was shown as a baby to the people in the theatre at Dublin. His birth would seem to have been too much for his mother, for she died the same year. Of Lord Talbot's two daughters, Fanny, the elder, married the 4th Earl of Dartmouth; her sister, Cecil, married the 7th Marquis of Lothian.

My grandfather's LIFE, written at nine years old as a present for his mother, shortly before her death, and evidently copied out for him by his sister Cecil, is an interesting document:

> As soon as I was born I was put under the care of Mrs King my nurse. I used to play all day in the nursery, then King thought it would be a good thing to teach me my A B C D and was very sorry to see me in convulsions. When I was five years old, I was put under the care of M. Petit Pierre who taught me my French Alphabet and all the French language. I beg your Excellency's pardon for not remembering how many times I have been to London. ('Your Excellency' was his mother.)

1

I thought London a very pretty town but there was a Square before our house that was very ugly. I like the country a great deal better than the town. Nice new milk instead of that nasty 'Milk below'.

In the country I walked down the New Road or round the Wood before breakfast; in London I only went to the nasty whey-shop in Hyde Park.

My master M. Petit Pierre was obliged to wait at dinner in London, which he was not in the country, except very seldom and those are the reasons for which I like Ingestre best. Papa went to France to try to find a house convenient to your Excellency and he did not succeed. Your Excellency went over to see France and both times Petit Pierre went away from me. Then I went to a little house belonging to Papa surnamed Birch Hall because there were a great many birch trees around it, which were used to flog and make blood come from the family.

When Petit Pierre came back from his travels I was greatly rejoiced, for I love him very much. I remember nothing since that till we went to Ireland where Papa was made Lord Lieutenant. I came with my sisters (for I have two sisters and seven brothers which I like tolerably well). We travelled through the country of Wales which is beautiful by its high and affecting mountains, till we got to Bangor ferry, which we passed with the greatest composure. Then we arrived at Holyhead; from there we climbed up into the Packet whose name is the *Unicorn*. We had a seven and a half hour passage. I was sick five times, Miss Bob 500 times (Miss Bob was the governess), Cecil 11 times and Fanny five times, but she was singing and laughing all the while. We landed at the Pigeon House and got into the Unicorn coach. We came galloping as hard as ever we could, but the Coachman was very cruel and clacked his whip and lashed his horses all the time. We passed through the fine city of Dublin, as last we arrived at the Phoenix Park, where, after a journey of four days, we found not one single crumb of bread, nor one tiny bit of meat; there were no beds prepared to refresh such poor tired people. At last the housekeeper, Mrs Rogers, a small little creature, found us two cups of tea. Fanny got a plate of cold mutton but she did not give me any and I went almost supperless to bed. Their Excellencies had been at Dublin for two days before us and arrived the next day at the Park. The Park is a fine place; there are a great many thorn trees and nut trees, and there are stags as well as deer. Now I must come back to the house. It is a nasty beggarly place for a Palace. It was a farm house but there were two wings put to it which made it look a little bit better.

I was placed in one of the wings. I went out on foot to view the Palace the day after I got there. At last I got a ride on Guzzy, who is my pony. She was beautiful at that time, grey and middling fat. I had a long ride round the Park and was greatly pleased with my ride. The Irish are such odd people; I did not know at first what to make of them. They are always pronouncing the words 'shure' and 'entoirely'. They are so cruel that they overload their horses. Fanny and Papa and Mama have seen one horse each killed by being overloaded and whipped.

Their cabins are as dirty and filthy as our nice little English cottages are clean.

I had the measles with all the family which we caught at the Hibernian Chapel. Petit Pierre took care of me in them and sat up with me eight nights without anybody changing him. The measles itched so that I was always tossing in my bed and I was all pimply and red. Then Mama and Papa went to the Castle. We staid at the Park and were left alone with good Thomas Newbold for our footman. P. Pierre had the care of the house to get it white-washed and repaired.

Once he made such an impression upon me in giving Jemmy Agram, the carpenter, a basin of beer that I shall never forget it. I went to the Castle five Sundays running and to the Buthnight and St Patrick's which I liked very much indeed.

Some time after Papa and Mama were come back from the Castle we went to Beau Parc.

It made me remember my own sweet country. It is beautiful. Long walks in the wood, the river Boyne at Bottom and Cascades and Lord Conygham's house and the stables and the lilacs and the bluebells made me like it very much, but we had all stinking beds and mine was so little and nasty it was impossible to bear it. As for Mr and Mrs Lambart (His grandfather and grandmother) I like them pretty well, only Mrs Lambart wears boots instead of shoes. Then we came back to the Park with tears in our eyes, we were so sorry to leave Beau Parc ...

I beg Mr Lear's pardon for not mentioning him before. He is a good charitable man and very active, because once when he dined at the Lodge he jumped out of his car which was trotting on, shut the door, leaped up the steps, and got into the house in one second. He teaches me to read English and to learn Latin and I like him pretty well. I go to him every day at the Royal Hospital, which is a fine building where live a great many miserable wretches. I come back to dine and sometimes after dinner Mr Carroll teaches me writing and arithmetic. This year we did not stay at the Park but went to the Castle with Papa and Mama. It is a pretty place; Papa built the front which makes it better than it was, though it was beautiful already. We have a nasty bedroom here and at first Petit Pierre had a bed full of fleas. There was a paillasse which the two Annes slept on the year before, but gave it him this year because it swarmed them with fleas. He soon turned it out and had a mattress made instead.

Then St Patrick's Day came again. I was in a box with Miss Bob and Cecil. It was a pretty sight to see 'em all dance and to see 'em enter. To be sure my head was a little turned next day for I did nothing well they said. The people were all drunk in Barrack St that day.

The band of some regiment or other comes into the Castle Yard every morning. They play two marches or airs whilst they're relieving the guard. I do nothing particular here.

Appendix by the author:

This work was accomplished with the greatest pain and work possible. I hope your Excellency will like it as well as my sister's presents because I had nothing to offer to you except my own composition and I hope next time I write my life it will be better and longer than it is now.
I remain your affect. and Dutiful son G.G.C. Talbot

Alas, there was no chance for Gustavus to give his mother another such present for she died that same year.

After the death of his wife, Lord Talbot had to bring up his large family of eight sons and two daughters as best he could. He was a conscientious man of religious feeling, and a staunch supporter of the Church of England. Perhaps this was the reason why he was reputed severe to Irish Catholics during his Lord Lieutenancy. His letter to his daughter Cecil, on her marriage in 1831 to Lord Lothian[1] gives sound parental advice and is typical of the religious feeling of the time. It recalls the father in Mrs Radcliffe's *Mysteries of Udolpho* who had 'too much good sense to prefer a charm to a virtue and had penetration enough to see that this charm was too dangerous to its possessor to be allowed the character of a blessing'.

My beloved – Most Beloved Child, – May Almighty God of His infinite mercy bless and preserve you. If you could but know how I love you. You have chosen a husband whom I now love for your sake, and shall soon learn to love for his own. Blessings upon you both, my

---

[1] John William Robert, 7th Marquis of Lothian

children. It would be proper for me to give you a word of advice, but to you advice is unnecessary. Continue your course already begun. Trust in God, my child, and He will never forsake you. Make Him the idol of your heart, recur to Him in all your difficulties, and whatever may be the storms of your life, He will bring you at last to a place of refuge.

After the Almighty, let your husband reign in your heart. You have now no duty but to obey him. Watch his looks and fulfil all his wishes, conform yourself to his habits and inclinations. Have but one mind, have no secrets from him. Be open, unreserved with him, reserved and cautious with all other men. Be cautious with female friends; remember that unless the persons you are thrown with are really good and religious, there is no dependence upon them. The married life is either one of happiness or misery, and much depends on the tact and conduct of the wife.

I ought now to thank you for your uniform, good, kind, and amiable conduct to me. You have made me happy. You have replaced your sainted mother. Imitate her, my child; never forget her virtues and you will prove a blessing to your husband. I have written more than I intended. My heart is full of joy, hope, grief, but, thank God, no fear. You will be happy, you will confer happiness. My future fate is in the hands of an Almighty and good God. May He, my beloved child, bless you with His best and choicest gifts. This is, ever will be, the prayer of your beloved father, for such I am proud to feel I am. God bless you, Cecil.

After her husband's death Cecil was converted to the Church of Rome, an event which caused a considerable stir at the time. Its reverberations may be felt in a letter from my great aunt, Caroline Talbot,[1] to my grandmother in 1851, typical of a certain kind of religious feeling:

The unhappy step which Cecil has taken, though no surprise, has been a great sorrow to us, though the change which her sentiments had undergone had for a long time past raised a barrier between us which had destroyed much of the comfort of our intercourse. Yet no such amount of separation prepares one to bear with indifference the positive and irremediable separation which the act itself establishes. We live in times of heavy distresses on the right hand and the left.

My grandfather Gustavus, the author of the LIFE, was sent to Charterhouse where he was at first bullied and unhappy. It was an

[1] Hon. Caroline Jane Stuart-Wortley, dau. 1st Lord Wharncliffe

unpleasant custom for the elder boys to dig up worms in the playground and force the younger boys to eat them. My mother often told me how my grandfather poured a jug of water into his bed at school, hoping that he would fall ill and be sent home; however, nothing of the kind resulted, and he remained perfectly well. Another story was of grandpapa and his brothers, at home at Ingestre for the holidays, harnessing saddle-horses to one of the carriages; the carriage turned over, my grandfather broke his leg, and this accident, it is said, prevented his going into the army ('The regiment I mean to be in'). Lord Talbot had a troublesome family to deal with.

From Charterhouse my grandfather went to Christ Church, Oxford, whence he was appointed to the living of Withington, but before being ordained, as was possible in those days. He read for orders with a Talbot uncle who was both a clergyman and a sportsman, for he was Master of the Meynell Hounds. It is told of this reverend M F H that he would read the evening service in top boots, so as to lose no time in getting to the place where the hounds were to meet on Monday morning.

Grandpapa went to Withington about 1836, and was ordained the year after, being then 23. The young clergyman was, probably, as well if not better known as a four-in-hand whip than as a preacher. As Halevy in his *History of the English People* in 1851 says, 'England was probably the sole country in Christendom where no proof of theological knowledge was extracted from candidates for ordination ...'.

The entrance examination once passed (it was elementary in the extreme, not to say childish), students who were not the eldest sons of gentle families, and had not the industry or capacity to take more difficult examinations, could proceed without further delay to the clerical status.

The village of Withington, in the county of Gloucester, lies retired in a shallow basin of the green Cotswold Hills, between Cheltenham and Cirencester. There is a windswept, wide air about the country, except in the sheltered village itself. The smooth, man-worked, beast-bitten finish of the valley, the very trees in the hedgerows, are the product of many centuries of cultivation. But the uplands which were once cornfields are now green pasture, and their greenness, if anything, adds to the timeless character of the landscape, whose features have altered little since the days when the Romans built their villa at Chedworth, or an earlier people travelled along the Fosseway. Even today the neighbourhood of Withington is unspoilt and rural. Farms, cottages and larger houses, all of stone, are grouped about, or dotted near the bed of the little river, which winds through the green meadows, with tufted willows overhanging the stream. The tall church tower rises out of a clump of trees.

The very name of Withington has a moss-grown sound to my ears. The Rectory, with is stone front, symmetrical and plain, its stone wings, the one older than the other, its garden of prim beds of geraniums, calceolarias and purple verbena, its round grass plot and sundial, had a certain dignity and seemliness. Built in the 17th and 18th centuries, it recalls that leisured age. The grandeur, it is true, is subdued and rustic, and the style grand only by comparison with surrounding cottages. It stands on high ground near the church, its windows looking down the valley and across the wooded slopes of Stowell Park, in my grandfather's day the property of Lord Eldon. The house, as I remember it as a child, was approached under a short avenue of yew trees from the village street, the church being on the left, the yew avenue making a boundary between the churchyard and the Rectory. The windows on one side of the house looked on to the churchyard, with its tombstones standing at all angles in the mossy turf.

The lower part of the Rectory domain was bounded in those days by a belt of tall trees, overhanging a walk of straggling yew, called the shrubbery (Cowperesque and melancholy to the backward-looking mind). Across part of the Rectory garden, spanned by two small arched bridges, ran a narrow sunken causeway, built by my grandfather to mask a right of way through the garden. The sunken path itself was narrow and sandy, and interesting to children were the voices of people passing along unseen, below the level of the ground. Its walls were covered with glossy ivy. Ivy, as well as yew, forms part of the Withington picture, twining among my childish memories. Ivy brings to mind a wonderful spider, shown me there by a boy cousin, among the dark shining leaves on the wall of the stone passage, purple and luminous in the middle of its web. The yew trees gave off a curious evergreen smell, mysterious, aromatic, and dim; and the fallen yew needles crackled dully under small feet. But best of all childish recollections is that of the bubbling spring in the upper part of the rough meadow the yew walk enclosed. What joy to small children to catch the drops, and even to bed one's mouth down to the leaping cold water itself!

Aunt Emma Talbot's photograph album has its ivy tendrils too – Aunt Emma who, before she died at 24 in 1876, wrote so many letters to her adoring sister Adela, to her own mother and to her two brothers, letters which still remain. Her album calls to mind Jane Eyre's vision at school of 'Sweet paintings of butterflies, hovering over unblown roses, of birds picking at ripe cherries, of wren's nests enclosing pearl-like eggs, wreathed about with young ivy sprays.'

At Withington my grandfather became acquainted with Emily Elwes, daughter of Squire Elwes of Colesbourne Park, only three miles distant, whom he married in 1843. And at Withington were born and brought up their five children, Emily, George, Emma, Gustavus and my mother, Adela.

A letter from Lord Talbot in 1843 shows the young couple newly installed at Withington:

> My dear Emily, Gustavus wants a Suffolk cart horse. I cannot afford to give him one, but this is no reason why I should not place a four year old filly at *your* feet to do as you like with. She, whom I call 'Eve', will be proud to belong to the Lady Rector of Withington Parish and there lead the *team* at the *farm*, as you do the Rector in all things (of which I approve most highly) in the house. (The Lady Rector was 22!) Gibbs has orders to deliver the mare to any person you may empower to receive her. May you long live to see this animal prosper under your auspices and protection. She really is a very fair specimen of Suffolk *horse* flesh. Good luck to you. I have had such pain since the wedding, in my left arm, that I have come to town for advice. Doctor Chambers says it is gout; although there are no outward indications of that savage malady. My trip to Scotland is therefore postponed if not altogether put by, this is very provoking, at present I see no prospect of being much better. (This journey was probably to have been to New Battle, the home of his daughter Lady Lothian.) But *I am better* I think generally speaking. Very affecty. Talbot.

Lord Talbot (who died in 1849) writes to Gustavus from Hereford in 1844:

> My dear Gustavus, Neither you nor I said one word of my coming to visit you and Emily. If therefore it should be perfectly convenient to you to let me come Wednesday 17 for a couple of nights, I will arrange plans accordingly ... Make no preparations for me. Peas or beans and bacon all I want for dinner, no soup certainly or salmon ... I must bring Dickens, as I am not able to dress myself alone. I shall drive to Ledbury, send my carriage home from there, post to you and the railway home (to Ingestre).

Another letter from Lord Talbot is more sentimental:

> My dear Emily, with many thanks have I to acknowledge the kind present of the spectacle case and the muffetees for your old pro papa. God bless you ma très chére fille and pray embrassez la jeune Emilie for me (the baby)... but if this is not sufficient I depute Gustavus, to whom my regards etc., as my deputy or proxy to embrace l'Emilie mère – Cunning bird, do not you sing so! I am in such a bother about gaiters (blue) I must end with you again thanking you my dear daughter.
>
> Ever T.

My grandfather lived at Withington for 62 years, and the Rectory seemed more like a country house than a parsonage, for his way of living was more that of squire than of a parson. His letters are full of horses and carriages, the state of the roads, and of shooting. He farmed an extensive glebe for many years and shot over his own land. When at Oxford in 1835 he had driven the coach from Oxford to London. His brother Gilbert writes many years after, 'It seems like a dream to remember the day when shortly after your taking possession of Withington you took me up on the "Magnet" or "Berkeley Hunt" to enter at Ch. Ch. in 1835, what old fellows we are.'

My grandfather was a great man with horses, easy going by nature, and inconsequent about money. He drove four-in-hand, a unicorn (three horses abreast), a pair or at least a single horse, to the end of his life at 86. He was a skilful whip and is remembered for managing a pair of horses, when the pole of the carriage broke, driving downhill, by keeping an even pace, with the use of brake and good hands, to prevent the carriage from running on to the horses.

Grandchildren remember him as an old man, seated high on the box of a double dog cart, driving a horse in single harness, a hard hat on his head and a black and white stock round his neck, with an onyx pin to keep it in place. The horse used to start with a touch of the whip, and the turn-out went round the drive in front of the house, down the yew walk, and away up the Cheltenham or Cirencester road. Sitting beside him, the small children felt grandpapa's power and familiarity in handing the ribbons. Those hands, in a sense ungraceful, yet seemed made for driving, the thumb rather turned up and the flat, wide fingers holding the reins lightly, the right hand balancing the whip with knowing skill. Clipperty-clop went the horse and carriage along the Cotswold roads.

Whitish yellow were those roads, winding through bare undulating country. On either side grew yarrow, and ragwort, while stone walls everywhere made boundary lines in the landscape. At the end of the outing the carriage bowled back through Withington village, down the little yew avenue, across the front of the house, and clattering on to stone cobbles, turned into the stable yard on the far side of the house. The old man would clamber down from the box and, mindful of his horse, give him a carrot or a lump of sugar. Stable yard, stone buildings, a gate; and then I think one could walk into the open field, with is thick tussocky grass and the pink seed like flowers of persicaria, growing rank by the pigsties of grey stone. The kitchen garden was behind, where we grandchildren spent August and September days digging our 'gardens', as certain bare patches by the wall were called. The smell of cabbage leaves, of apples or mignonette in the sun will always remind me of that walled-in little kitchen garden.

Lower down, some three fields away, the brook wandered between banks, where water forget-me-knot and loose-strife grew, and where sweet briar and water-mint gave their own never-to-be-forgotten smell. In May and June lily-of-the-valley grew in the woods, and my mother, Adela, would gather the sweet-smelling things and post bunches of them to her friends.

In June and July the haymakers used to be at work in the fields. I remember the haycocks below the railway line that crossed the fields and labourers and boys drinking tea, sent from the Rectory, out of their cans. Late in the summer came the school feast, with excited children, dressed in thick homemade clothes, thick boots and pinafores, running races and calling out in the sing-song Gloucestershire dialect, or sitting on benches, munching bread and jam and drinking tea out of the mugs they had brought with them. 'Lower End' was a part of the village that one reached by walking down the fields across the stream on a plank bridge under the small brick railway arch over which the antiquated engine drew its little old-fashioned carriages. To walk to 'Lower End' by the road was called going 'oop strit' in Gloucestershire dialect. 'B'est gioing oop strit?'

Beyond 'Lower End', over bare-looking plough land and pasture, stretched the road to Northleach, bordered with stone walls, and up this road grandpapa used to drive to carry out his duties as magistrate and guardian. Today the surrounding fields are green and dappled with livestock. It is still so rural that only the little railway reminds one of modern life, so peaceful that the traveller who returns after many years sees little change. Half-way along that road was Dancer's farm with its white crochet antimacassars and red woollen mats on the table where we went to visit Mrs and the Miss Dancers. And in 'Lower End' itself lived old John Winter, with his smock frock, and Ellen Laight the old washerwoman, whose goffered bonnet framed her lined and smiling face.

The legend of Withington is made up in my mind of the stories my mother used to tell of childhood and young ladyhood, as well as my own early memories; of the moss house Algy Elwes made for the kitten in the shrubbery; of the French governess who told her to lift up her crinoline, when walking downstairs, to prevent it clanking on every step; of the dog 'Wasp' who ate her doll; of the Elwes family walking over from Colesbourne to afternoon church; and later of the illness of her sister Emma and of her death at Ventnor. And in the same year came grandmama's death, and then grandpapa's money troubles over farms and horse dealers, and the difficult part my mother had to play as the only child left at home. The writing of letters then was an important part of life; the writing table, the wooden writing-case, the pens, the pen-wipers had and still have a vital interest of their own.

Sorting the bundles of old letters, in the thin criss-crossed handwriting, turning out the boxes of ribbons, check, tartan, moiré, and 'Roman', the drawers of little curled ostrich feathers, the boxes of fans, the silk and lace scarves, orris-root and bitter-apple among them, all this brings Withington before me. Through the rustling of the papers, as I seem to brush them aside in clouds, I see the grey front of the house, and, inside it, the cases of bright stuffed birds, the polished oak staircase, curving upwards, the dining room to the left, with jasmine outside the window, the sunny drawing room upstairs with its round table and cross-stitch chair, and petit point fire screen and the bare echoing stone passages of the back parts of the house. A special aroma belongs to it all, of pot-pourri, dried flowers, and old prayer books; the crushed hopes, and all subdued to the outlook of a country rectory, mellowed, as it were, by church services, by the curious mixed poetry of the hymn book, and the dignity of the Anglican ritual.

One of my grandmother's letters to my mother, who was away at the Elwes' at Colesbourne, describing a winter's journey, brings a picture of snow at Withington and cold Cotswold weather:

Withington, Jan. 22

Dearest Adela,

You see I am come home. We went a great part of the way fr. Chelt. at a foot's pace, but otherwise we got on pretty well, tho' it was hard work for the horses. There was not much snow round Worcester, or indeed lower down than Gaines, but it was very deep at Chel. and the higher we got the worse it was. I am glad you did not come home in such dismal weather. Our shrubs at the end of the stables, and the opposite clump, are terribly split and broken, some will not recover. The rockery at Brockhampton was strewed with branches, and one scotch fir out of a clump of three, below the house, is quite knocked down. I wonder when I shall see you. I could not get yr. crepelisse at Cheltm. today, because the High St was so slippery that Papa would not go that way, but went by the College. Emily (my mother's eldest sister, Mrs Lutley) and John wished me to stay, but I wd. not let Papa come home alone. Yr. Blk. jacket is here, I have not ventured to open it, and I do not send it by post boy, because it is hard enough for him to travel without it. Love to Aunt M. etc.

I am ever yr. affect. Mother E.S.T.

Another letter, written from London, by my grandmother, describes the coming of the branch railway line, the North Cotswold Railway, to that rural valley:

41 Portman Sqr., July 15 '64

Dearest Adela,

You know that our railway bill has passed the House of Lords, and we shall really have a railway through Withington. We shall come home tomorrow, *all* of us, and I think we shall not arrive till soon after seven and three quarters, so you need not expect us before that. I suppose the Withington people are very glad to hear about the railway. The weather has been so dry that I do not expect the garden to look well, but I *do* expect the *grass* mown, in the ring and also the shrubbery. Last night we went to the Opera, which we liked very much, and tonight we go to a ball. Tell Maria we shall want our dinner about half past seven, and we should like two ducks, and a red currant tart. Never mind about the ducks, if they are not killed, we can have some mutton. I suppose the poor people have had some soup?

Tell Elizabeth (the housemaid) I hope she will have done all her cleaning before we get home, and you must sleep in my room. Tell Emma I got her letter this morning, and it was very well written.

Believe me ever yr. affecate. Mother.

Emily S. Talbot

Another of my grandmother's letters, written from Brockhampton, the Lutleys, is very precise in its directions. She was presiding at the birth of one of her sister-in-law, Emily Lutley's children. Adela was only twelve.

> Dearest Adela,
>
> When the bureau is unlocked at breakfast time, look under the box of toothpicks and you will see the key of the *Kitchen Clock*, give it to Curtis (the butler) for Monday is the day to wind it up; and near that key is the key of the schoolroom tea chest, which put in your pocket. Take the housekeeping keys to Sarah, unlock the cupboards and she will take out what she wants. Tell Hannah she must take up a kettle for yr. tea in the schoolroom, and you must put out some schoolroom candles, Sarah knows the key, it is with the others, the smallest; and order two eggs for tea tomorrow, one for Mademoiselle, and tell Hannah to take up her supper just before nine, cold meat and bread and a potatoe, and a glass of beer, on a tray, with a small napkin on it. You may get six Normandy pippins out, and have them for your dinner on Tuesday, they must be cooked on Monday. A beautiful pot of lilies of the valley, in blossom in the drawing room here. No time for more.
>
> Ever yr. affectate Mother Emily S. Talbot

Little Adela, dressed like a Tenniel 'Alice' in the photographs, was proud enough no doubt to carry out all these instructions. My grandmother writes to Adela again from Malvern, in 1869:

> Emily has in the drawing room soup plates with four or five roots of primroses planted in each, the earth is then covered with moss and they blossom and last so well. Have you watered the plants in the drawing room? Give Hudson the sleeves of the shirt, which is in my work basket, and ask Sarah to write down the weight of the last sheep, and when she has any candles out as Mlle. to put it down on a piece of paper and keep it for me. Is there any soup for the poor people?

It was the time of the Franco-Prussian War. But rural England, with its housekeeping and railway making, and thoughts of soup for the poor people, was not much affected by it.

Emma's letter from London in 1871 shows the undying interest in clothes felt by the Withington family and delight in concerts and gaieties.

> Theresa has ordered two bonnets, one is 10s. and another white chip
> with tulle and two white feathers 28s. On Saturday Jane is going to
> take me to a grand morning concert at the Floral Hall, where Patti,
> Mario, Pauline Lucca, Faure and loads of others are to sing and
> Arabella Goddard to play. I am sorry you do not like your bonnet,
> black is very much worn this year, the strings tie under your chin and
> the tulle ones tie or pin also under the chin. Tell Adela that all the hats
> I have seen are small, with highish crowns and flat brims and nearly
> all trimmed with two or three rows of velvet or ribbon and lace, with
> a bow and general muddle at the side.

Patti and Florio and the Floral Hall and the latest bonnets in London
were great news at Withington, but Adela, too, has something to tell.
She writes in 1872: 'Has Papa told you the glorious news that Curtis has
caught the mouse in the drawing room that has for the last week been
frightening me out of my wits?' My grandmother writes to Adela who
was staying with old Miss Jane Talbot at Temple Guiting:

> I am sure you have been out with the shooters today, it has been lovely.
> I went out at 10.30 and divided polyanthus and auricular roots, and
> then the organ, and more gardening since luncheon... This place has
> been alive all day, the hounds at Foss Bridge and people shooting the
> woods etc all day... I have written to a man at Cheltenham to come
> and inspect the church stove.

A summer's day is evoked by Emma's letter in 1873, to her mother
who is away, describing Adela's 17th birthday at Withington on August
9th: 'They all seemed to enjoy themselves. I was dressed a few minutes
after eight and went out and got Adela a bouquet of carnations and
jasmine.' One can well imagine Emma flitting out of the double door
in the summer morning air, picking the jasmine from the front of the
house, and making a bunch of it with carnations from the kitchen
garden. Another letter, in winter, from Emma to her absent mother,
relates to money worries which, one feels, weighed sadly upon the
young housekeeper. With her ill health, Emma was evidently inclined to
be anxious. Perhaps papa is outside looking at the horses in the stable; it
is dark in the drawing room. Emma has only one candle on the writing
table:

> I have not much to tell you except that we are very well and flourishing.
> We have finished our embroidery. I am rather sorry it's done. Such a
> wet night, it is very black and cloudy still, but not actually raining.

Papa gave me one pound to go to Cirencester. I hope I shall get something settled about money as he says he won't pay for any of our clothes now that you have your money and unless you do it I don't quite see my way to getting dressed on my large income of £1 6s. per annum! It is such a bore having a little row over every bill. I have got to hate the sight of them, but I can't help their coming for I do my best to spend as little as I can, as you know. The little bellows have at last come to an untimely end. I blew up the fire this morning and the 'nozzle' fell right off, so they are concluded. When are you coming home? Your loving child, Emma F. Talbot

Perhaps the poignancy of the letters lies in the evidence of the quietness of life at Withington. Quiet it certainly was, at home; but when the daughters went away they generally visited grand relations. Then they were often hard to put it to devise dresses suitable for such occasions.

To reduce everyone's possessions to the same level is perhaps too logical. Drama and contrast man demands and these had their particular form in Victorian England in the relationship between rich and poor. No doubt the Miss Talbots' lives gained interest by contriving kindness to the latter and by holding their own in dress with the former, an antithesis which reminds one of Blake's 'Human Abstract':

Pity would be no more
If we did not make somebody poor;
And mercy no more could be
If we all were as happy as we.

Letters from Adela, who went to London for the first time at the age of 16 in 1874, tell of her going to concerts and the Opera:

The Handel Festival was more charmingly delightful than I expected. We had to dress as quickly as possible to go to dinner with the de Wintons ... Trebelli was so charming in blue satin as Cherubini last night and a new one, Marie Rose, was Susanna; she is very pretty indeed and has a good voice, though it seemed rather husky. Titiens as the Countess wore some lovely gowns and sang very well but she is so ugly and her top notes screamed rather.

In 1875 Adela writes from Alton Towers (the Shrewsburys), evidently enjoying the gay life and half forgetting for the time being Emma's illness, which was causing anxiety at home. To Adela, who used to embroider her dresses at home, those of the married ladies at Alton would seem very grand. A letter I have lost describes the fifteen flounces added to a last year's Paris gown of Theresa, Lady Shrewsbury, for the Stafford Ball; another is about hats:

> 5 January
> Dear Mama, would you mind sending me my hard felt billy-cock hat, as the feathers on my other hat will get spoilt if I am out in the damp with it on. These girls (Nelly Talbot, and her two sisters) go out in theirs every day and they look so nice ... I am going to wear my black gown with very light blue ribbon and real holly for the Stafford Ball.

Emma was ordered to go to the Isle of Wight for the winter, on account of her health. Another letter, written to cheer the two sisters at Ventnor, is from Mrs John Henry Elwes, describing the re-opening of Withington Church after restoration:

> The whole service so nice. No fussy display as in some churches. Your dear old daddy looked so nice and so kind and I am sure performed his part beautifully... And your mother looked so well and her bonnet suited her, you can't think how nice she looked.

One can hear the rustling of silk dresses, the whispering, and the handing round of prayer books. One fancies the mild satisfaction of those present, the nods, and then the luncheon that followed in the school.

Elegance, different from that of the 18th century, different from Edwardian smartness, different from University culture, was fostered in these Victorian days by the education, the French governesses and the lingering remnants of deportment. Social distinctions and barriers reinforced this elegance, and Christian principles, to some extent, softened its austerity. Soup, puddings in the china jars encased in basket work, visits, interest, curiosity even, were the current coin of kindness to the 'poor people', as they were called.

At Withington, cottages were of stone, thatched or tiled, the front door opening straight into the kitchen. Most of the parishioners were farmers or farm labourers, shepherds, or stockmen. In the '60s and '70s they were poor, though in earlier days they had been even poorer. Old John Winter's story of the baker, told to my mother and myself when a child, shows what life could be like for labourers in the hungry 'forties.

In his smock frock, with the rheumy eye and toothless gums of the old yokel, John Winter told us, in a quavering voice, how many years before, when he and his wife had 'nor bread nor money nor marbles' and a family to feed, and he had gone out 'by moonshoine for ter dig up turmuts for som'at t'eat and the baker, 'e comes driving along the roa'ad in 'is cart and 'e say "what b'est doin' there John?" and a tells 'e I've nor bread, nor money, nor marbles. Well 'e goes 'ome and the nex' mornin' there was six loaves on the doorstep' – so John told me in triumph. But it didn't always end like that.

My mother seldom went to sleep at night, in winter at least, without thinking about the poor. She began her training early, for in 1862 when she was six years old, she writes in a childish hand to her own mother, 'Emma and I gleaned for Hannah Winter, she was so pleased, if it's fine we shall go again in the fields and glean for her. Mademoiselle wishes to be kindly remembered to you.'

As children, my mother used to sing to us, and with gusto, the Valentine song which Withington children were in the habit of singing on St Valentine's Day, at the door of the Rectory:

> Marnin' marnin' Valentoine,
> Oi be ragged and you be foine,
> So plaize to give me a valentoine,
> Roses red and violets blue,
> Carnations sweet and so be you,
> And so good morrow Valentoine,
> Throw the oats agin the woine,
> Oi be ragged and you be foine,
> So plaize to give me a valentoine.

She remembered the mummers too, in winter, and would describe how the man with the bladder chased her as a little girl along the servants' passage, frightening her very much.

In October 1876, my grandfather writes to his daughter Adela: 'Yesterday was a terrible day of all the poor farm servants to move to their new places, they must have got all their bedding and children wet. You will find the garden pulled to pieces.' A Michaelmas picture indeed; and my grandmother in 1861 writes:

> We had a most prosperous Xmas day and a bright frost and sun for giving away the bread and cheese. Henry Elwes, Eddy and Alex Campbell came over for evening church. Adela danced the quadrille nearly every day with Emma and me, and knows the first three, but she would not dance last night, and sat on my lap nearly all the evening (at Colesbourne).

Emma's letter in 1871 gives a picture of illness in the village:

> In the afternoon I went round the village and was not tired. I went
> to Barnfields and found Eliza not quite so well. She was downstairs
> but sitting up makes her so faint and sick, and she had nothing but a
> common wooden chair, so I have extracted the poor people's chair
> from the Smiths, who have kept it ever since Mrs Smith died, and I
> am going to send it down to the Barnfields.

Is it not possible that a 'dull' life, as it is called, with a little movement, can yield pleasures as well as a life of gaiety? That, fed at its spring by hope and affection, the heart, like a winding river, makes its own course? For changes of weather and season, longings for the unknown, fears even, give colour and movement; letters and books, gardening, sport, and pets give variety to such a life as that lived at Withington. Time could hang heavy there, as the letters show, but life was generally full enough, of carriages coming round, letters from the outer world, from London, from Rome, from Ingestre, or Temple Guiting; of the leaves coming off, illnesses of cottagers, dresses made at home, shopping at Cheltenham, driving over to Colesbourne.

Yet was it so quiet after all? For there were the visits – someone was always leaving Withington for Brockhampton in Worcestershire, or Alton, Lord Shrewsbury's great house, or Patshull and the Legge cousins. At these houses the big parties assembled, the young ladies and their mothers, young men destined to become friends or admirers, whose photographs were duly enshrined in Emma's album, with ivy tendrils, jasmine or maidenhair fern painted round them. These were all described and criticised by the two sisters in writing to one another, sometimes kindly, sometimes unkindly – and these visits had great importance to the family at Withington, especially to my grandmother, who combined a certain guileless snobbishness with her practical good sense.

Emma went to Cannes and to Florence and Rome in 1866 and 1867, and spent a season in London in 1871. George went to school in Brussels and later Gussy went to Ceylon. And over the course of years people returned, were met at Cirencester in the 'Basket', or stopped at Cheltenham to buy a winter petticoat.

Two

GRANDPARENTS

Except for his friend Lord Canning, who became Viceroy of India, and had been with him at Oxford, and for his own relations, I fancy my grandfather was more at home with horses than with men. Tall and loosely built, he had a good-natured, aristocratic air, with an aquiline nose, rather watery grey eyes, a finely shaped high forehead and a long chin. He had a statesman-like look, but whether from association of the mind with persons of that type, or from latent nobility in himself, I cannot say. Though driving and care of horses was his great interest, he did his duties as rector in an easy-going fashion, looking after his parishioners with the kind-hearted sense of duty he had learnt from his father. He was taken for granted by his people. 'For', said one of them when he had been at Withington for 60-odd years, 'we have had the Honourable with us so long, we could not do with anybody else.'

A story is told, either of my grandfather or another Gloucestershire rector, about a tiny church which had a service only once a month. When the day arrived, the farmer's wife begged the rector to preach from anywhere but the pulpit, as her hen-turkey had chosen to lay there and was even then sitting on her eggs.

My grandfather, my mother said, never asked a parishioner into his house, but he would walk up and down in front of the Rectory talking to anyone who came to see him. He took the services every Sunday, usually preaching a sermon. When he became old and childish a curate took the duty, and I remember seeing my grandfather's surplice and cassock hung up in a wardrobe out of sight, hidden in fact by my mother, who was afraid Grandpapa might take it into his head to put them on and take part in the service. He used to call us children 'my poppets' and give us slices of sponge cake as a treat. It is true that a sharp-tongued critic described him doing little but poke up the weeds with his spud, fill his pipe and feel the horses' legs, but that was in his old age. His earlier letters display the normal rural activity of a 'squarson' in the village and on the Bench.

A letter to my grandmother shows him after attending a great church ceremony:

> Ingrestre 1861
>
> My dearest old Mummy, well, all the ecclesiastical work is over [he writes with evident relief]. I never saw such a magnificent sight as yesterday at Lichfield, four bishops, 300 clergy, and the cathedral, which is magnificent, so crowded that there was not standing room ... we lunched at the Deanery and got home at 8.30. I drove the bus and three horses abreast, we changed at Rugely. It was very dark coming home and I did not know the road, not having been on it for 30 years but we got home alright ... [His eldest daughter is with him and a party of young cousins in the house.] Emily is gone out riding on 'Rosamund' with Jessie, Arthur, and Charley [Gerald] who arrived last night from Ireland. Walter also came at 2 a.m. this morning from Blickling, he says that Concy was so sorry not to have you and gives a bad account of Lothian ... Pat went to Knowesley yesterday. Shrewsbury goes to London tonight, back tomorrow, Arthur on Friday to meet the Bishop of Oxford. He wants me to go.
>
> Ever affectionate, G.G.C. Talbot

Lord Canning's death caused my grandfather some regret; he writes in 1862 from:

> 28 Parliament Street, Westminster
>
> My Dearest Mummy, Poor dear Canning is no more! He died at six this morning. I feel it very much but not so much as I should have done had he not been away for so many years. The last I know of him was that Granville saw him yesterday at 3 p.m. and he [Canning] just knew him. He is a great loss both nationally and to me personally on account of Georgy. I found nobody in Belgrave Square. Shrewsbury was out and the girls are at Richmond. So I dined at the Wellington. I went to Portman Square in the evening. [This was the town house of the Elwes' where my grandmother had spent much of her youth. Then there was Aunt Caroline (Mrs John Talbot) who, though rather alarming, kept open house for many nephews and nieces.] I saw Caroline in the street this morning and asked if she thought Johnny would take in Gussy for his Exeat and the Exhibition ... I wrote to Cecil and Pat last night to ask them if they would give me dinner tonight. I must go and get their answers.

I can imagine Grandpapa with his tall figure and awkward walk, going round the family houses in London and ringing the front door bells.

Sometimes when Grandpapa went back to Ingestre, he fell back into the easy ways of the great country house where he had been brought up, and found it hard to tear himself away from the riding and shooting, even when Emily was alone and the children were sick. He sounds a little conscience-stricken.

> Ingestre
>
> We have just been into Stafford and I had your letter by the 2nd post. I am so sorry that you should have so much anxiety about the children, and should be all alone. I trust they are all better now. It is just the same thing as everybody has here. We had a delightful ride this morning, about 15 miles on Cannock Chase. If I had been quite well I should have enjoyed it amazingly. I am just going to shoot wild ducks in Tixall Park. I thought I would not come home. I was so unwell – Poor Mummy I am sorry that you are all alone. I have quantities of sugar plums for the children.
>
> Ever Affec. Hubby, G.G.C. Talbot

Living in one spot throws less strain on the personality than moving from place to place, for background and character grow into one another. Preoccupations become fixed, habits engrained, idiosyncrasies marked. Prejudice enriches the narrow fields of its scope. The elaborate patterns thrown out by a frame of mind expand like ice flowers on a window pane. The state of relative timelessness is reached, in which the regular rhythm of occupations is felt.

It is worth noting that Victorian England, with its fixed conventions, besides its great novelists, Dickens, Trollope, Thackeray, George Eiot, The Brontës, Disraeli and the rest, and its illustrators, Cruikshank, Leech and Dicky Doyle, had Lewis Carroll and Edward Lear to make fun of its routine and its prejudice and to turn its solemnities upside down, while Victorian Scotland had, in George Macdonald and later Barrie, makers of satisfying fantasies, fountains to refresh its somewhat arid soil. In such ways as this the unexplained, the unmentionable, the infantile side of things are not left without a witness and find singular outlets; the gaps left by common sense and good taste are sometimes filled by nonsense.

Snobbishness, pride of purse, sectarianism, are the obverse side of the bright medal of tradition, the ugly and the common part of the framework which keeps the body politic together. Disraeli saw this and exemplified it in his novels. He makes Coningsby say: 'Let me see authority once more honoured, a solemn reverence again the habit of our lives; let me see property acknowledging, as in the days of faith, that labour is his brother, and that the essence of all tenure is the performance of duty.'

My grandmother was a true Elwes. She had large blue eyes, was of middle height and had a certain elegance of person. She managed the parish with energy, had a caustic tongue, wrote numerous letters, and took a great interest in the garden. Her brother's home at Colesbourne, three miles away, had been her own home, and in it she sometimes once more became her youthful, her absurd, and her quizzical self.

On one occasion when John Henry Elwes, her brother, had told her he was going abroad for a change, she remarked, 'a change of smells I suppose!' For Uncle John Henry used to return from his travels and complain of the smells he had met with. On another, when a somewhat pompous and touchy lady who was dining at Colesbourne, displayed a fine lace shawl she had brought back from abroad and bragged of their Spanish port, my grandmother, to the horror of her relations, picked up an antimacassar from one of the chairs and, draping it round her shoulders, walked up and down the room saying, 'Look at my beautiful Spanish lace shawl, its just come from Spain in six barrels!' Perhaps the effort of being the 'Lady Rector' of Withington made a return to childhood's ways when at Colesbourne both a relief and a necessity.

She was a good French scholar, and her sons used to make fun of her constant use of French, ascribing to her an imaginary sentence about 'Taking a journey to "Tuticorin" dressed in "Tarlatan" with my feet in a chanceliere.' To me she seems a true Victorian, of regular habits, practical, 'bien elevée', unsentimental, conventional, but with the delicate sense of the ridiculous that conventionality fosters, and the avid interest in detail a monotonous life begets in women, when facts about people, their clothes, engagements, remarks, incomes seem to scintillate, endlessly changing, like motes in a sunbeam. In summer, she would sit in the garden at Withington, sewing, her eyes shaded by a curious bonnet called an 'Ugly'. Asked by a visitor whether she had seen a certain entertainment in London, she replied with asperity, 'I live at Withington, I sew pinafores!'

Her letters, written in the elegant and precise handwriting of the day, are clear in the matter of household direction, and show something of the gardener and naturalist. In 1869 my grandmother writes to Emma:

> The doctor says you are to pass the winter in a warm locality, which
> I conclude must mean Torquay, which, I am sure, you will find more
> lively than Withington. I have spent 24 whole winters here, and
> therefore am a pretty good judge – tell me what you thing about
> going to Torquay? I wish you would write to Adela and give her some
> advice about a winter frock, for she ought to have one, but I can't
> persuade her to choose one at Cheltenham, nor do I know how to
> advise her to have it made. Adela is very dull and hopes Emma will
> come soon.
>
>   Ever your affec. Mother, Emily S. Talbot

Had she too much power of endurance or was this virtue in the inevitable
fate of her generation?

She writes constantly about plants and flowers; as for instance in
March 1876, to Adela at Kirby Fleetham, Lord and Lady Castlereagh's:

> Yesterday we had a heavy thunderstorm and a great deal of rain, as
> Wright said – 'the h' air was full of lightning'. Today a bright fine
> morning – the poor little Lent lilies are quite out, but the hail and
> rain yesterday nearly knocked them down, but luckily I had propped
> them with sticks. Do you think you will be able to drive to Bedale
> to look for the primula farinose? You will never again have such a
> chance, though it is not easy to drive to an unknown field and march
> over it.

There was nothing slipshod about the Victorians. Both the regular
habits and the careful handwork that went to the making of their dresses
had something satisfying about them and helped to give shape to the
succession of their days.

Perhaps an irritable heart sharpened her tongue. No doubt the
Victorian costume, the stays, the heavy skirts and petticoats, were
unconsciously trying to delicate women. And though the undeviating
regularity made a secure framework to life, yet keeping up the routine
may well have been too much for her, for she died of a heart ailment at
forty-five.

Lord Talbot kept up with Withington till he died in 1849. And
Lady Sarah Ingestre, daughter of the Marquis of Waterford and wife
of Lond Ingestre, my grandfather's brother, wrote many letters to my
grandmother, some about their various children, others relating to
journeys in Ireland to visit her relations in the Beresfords, and others

again on life in London and the Court functions. She writes from Bute House, Old Brompton, one of the country houses which still stood on the edge of Hyde Park:

> May '49
>
> I must take time to write you a line my dear Emily ... As yet there has not been much gaiety, but there seems a burst this week, of parties, as well as of the May, which is now in full bloom in my little garden, and I could almost fancy myself this morning as peaceful as you are at Withington. But soon people will be coming to visit, and tomorrow we dine at Lady Salisbury's, a ball afterwards, Wednesday, another dinner, and things in the evening. Friday, Duke of Devonshire's, Saturday dine at Lord Rosebery's, Lady Peel afterwards. Pretty well for a quiet character like me if I do all this in one week, which I doubt very much under circumstances existing... I saw Lady Canning the other day looking very well, but I think out of spirits about her father, although she does not own it. The steamer is just gone for them. The Waterfords came over to meet them about the 25th.

(Now come some confidences about births in the family.)

> I am hourly now expecting the first Beresford child of *this* generation. Lady Jonny is looking so well, poor little dear, she little knows *what it is*!! (!) But *bad* as the affair is of having *animals*, one cannot help wishing (for) them for oneself and others. I am glad Emily had cut her teeth so well. I have not yet seen Caroline's baby. I believe it is quite a *Talbot* in size. Cecil [Lady Lothian] dined here today with Pat and Gilly. I was so glad to see her comfortably, I think her looking very well, and it was a great pleasure to have her to myself. We *used* to be such friends, though separation, time and circumstances may have made us less intimate of late years, still I am always ready *to warm up* when we get together. My Lord wants us to run to Ingestre for Whitsuntide, but I cannot manage it. I hope we may be there in the summer, as he wants us to be at Ingestre after *my affair*, if all goes well. I am not nervous about the business except at times, when I think, though *not probable*, still it is possible that all may not go well. Perhaps this is wrong as well as foolish, but still I have so many interests now that make me feel I should be sorry to have to leave them, and it is difficult to attain to that state of preparation which I always think one ought to be in (when there is even a remote chance of danger) indeed at all times, if one did not cling too much to one's earthly blessings. What a lecture I am writing to you, but I enjoy a good chatter with you and I let my pen run on as my tongue does

or did when we were together, I assure you I liked my visit to you quite as much, if not more than you could, and often think of how snug we were together. I hope you may be at Ingestre if we are there in the Summer. Ingestre likes the *greys* very much. [My grandfather seems to have been entrusted with the buying of a pair of horses.] At first we thought they would not look well with our yellow carriage, but Ingestre was determined to buy them, as he said it was hard on Gustavus to have them so long in London, and our open carriage is to be painted again *dark* that we may look well. I do not think they look amiss in the yellow one, although I believe it is contrary to the *strict rule*.

I must mention the *hens*, the poor black on died almost immediately, but the others are well and laying daily. We have not quite, though *nearly* settled about taking Brompton Park now, but I think we shall sooner or later. I went to Brighton the other day to see Walter, I think the sea air agrees with him, and as much as I could judge of Mrs Walker I liked her and her school. I never saw a boy so improved in looks as Arthur's Charley. My own Charley was here for two days on his return to Eton. '*He is a* Talbot', and looks 16 instead of 14! ... He likes Eton and I trust will do well there ... Kiss Emily for me, and the girls, they often talk of her.

Ever your affec. Sister, Sarah Ingestre

An interesting glimpse of Queen Victoria and festivities at Windsor appears in another letter from Brompton Park dated 12 June 1849:

My dear Emily,

All you say about Pussy is most kind. How I wish you were in London to be at your sister's Ball, but you always think of Gustavus's interests and avoid all expense of journeys for his sake, never regarding your own pleasures; it would be well for every poor man if their wife was like you. I hear there is every prospect of your sister's ball being a good one. We have an engagement to Lady Wilton the same night, but we must manage to do both for once in a way. This life does not suit me, but as Pussy [Lady Victoria Talbot] gets on very well, I do not dislike it as much as I should in any other case. We had a pleasant week at the Deanery at Windsor, Ascot two days, and two dances at the Castle, the Queen going up and down a country dance of nearly 80 people, and in such spirits. There never was so happy a Queen, and seldom so happy a woman as she is. I think of going to Ingestre from Saturday to Tuesday as Concy is to be confirmed at Stafford on *Monday*.

Three

THE FAMILY AT WITHINGTON

Of the Withington family, which consisted of Emily, George, Emma, Gussy and Adela, Emily the eldest, born in 1844, was tall and handsome. She went out a good deal as a young lady and was much admired at the County Balls. She married her cousin, John Lutley of Brockhampton, in 1864.

Brockhampton is a typical country seat in Worcestershire, a late 18th-century red brick house set on a tiny plateau, its windows overlooking a panorama of hills and dales, with a rolling park where fine beeches and oaks toss their branches and overhang the two approaches. Up these grandpapa used to often drive his pair of horses to visit his eldest daughter. During the illness and after the death of the handsome Emily, who died in 1884, he would drive his youngest daughter, Adela, the fifty or so miles from Withington to visit John Lutley and his children.

I like to picture them going up the steep hill over Bringsty Common at a foot's pace on a summer's evening as the light touched the Malvern Hills, and the bracken and gorse stood out in pointed distinctness. The horses would hearten up as they entered Brockhampton lodge gates and would trot sedately along the curving drive under the low and sweeping beeches till the carriage came to a halt in front of Brockhampton itself. My mother must often have stood gazing into the distance as she alighted, over Knightswick Hill and across to the Welsh Border, as she returned again and again to stay at hospitable Brockhampton. The old family house, Lower Brockhampton, lies cupped in green hills and hidden in woods, a 14th-century manor house built of grey oak timbers and yellow plaster, rosy brick and stone, standing on an island surrounded by a brimming moat, with a little black and white moat house with iron studded door guarding the bridge. A small roofless stone chapel stands beside it, farm buildings in front and, across the moat, an orchard of apple trees in rows.

Quiet it lies, belonging to the past, a manor for one of Shakespeare's gentlemen – a moated grange for Mariana.

Next in the family came George, a good-looking boy who grew up to be an Olympian figure of six foot seven with auburn beard and blue eyes. His ill-written, boyish letters give an idea of school life at Rugby in the 'sixties.

> Rugby 1860
>
> Dear Papa, the pads cost 10s. 6d. I want them especially as I have been hit on my bone with a ball which does not do it any good I assure you – when I wanted to play an end and saw all the other boys with balls and stumps and who could not lend me, I had nothing to do except stand and watch or read in the study which looks on to the Close, so I do hope you will send it soon as I have nothing to do … the rooks are building in the Close, they make an awful noise.

George went to Brussels for two years in 1862. His letter to Emily in 1863 describes how

> I saw the Princess Alexandra arrive and was close up to the carriage – she looked very tired. She did not go to the Opera. Jenkins (the crammer) gave us leave to go but I didn't, as I thought she wouldn't appear … I hope it will be fine for the marriage … I have only two flannel shirts and one is out at the elbows.

On his return from Brussels George went on the Cotton Exchange at Liverpool, whence he writes: 'I was nearly buying Papa some cotton yesterday … and now the market is wild – all depends on the American news on Monday, when, if Lincoln is elected, we shall have fair sailing and good prices for some time.'

And in May 1864 he describes town life and the huge meals of the well-to-do:

> I like Liverpool much better now than I did, as I know more people and generally go somewhere or other from Saturday till Monday, so my life is not so monotonous as I thought it would be. I have plenty to do in the day, but always manage to get away by five, and go to cricket every night. We've quite a swell club here with three professionals and 240 members; we played our opening match yesterday, and had a heavy dinner afterwards. I began my career by making the respectable score of 5 … I stayed at Knowsley the last two Sundays with the Hornbys, Lord Derby's cousin and agent, he's a

very nice fellow, and has some pretty daughters. I don't know what
I should do if I couldn't get away generally on Sundays, as its horrid
work here. The routine is as follows – after church, go a walk on
the landing stage for an appetite, then if you are asked anywhere for
dinner, you begin to gorge at 1 p.m. at a stiff dinner of soup and
fish three or four courses, cheese, dessert, and wine after the ladies
are gone, which lasts till about half past three, then we congregate
together and attempt a walk which is not of long duration as everyone
is so full he can hardly move, so we generally 'drop in' to someone's
lodgings where we talk and smoke till church time at 6, when of
course, after eating so much we go to sleep. After church go to your
friends house to tea and after that look in to someone else's lodgings
till ten when there is a heavy supper of meat, beer, bread and cheese
and wine. By this time you can't eat any more and go home to bed,
and sleep off the effects, and on Monday morning are quite seedy, so
it's a mercy to ask me into the country for the Sunday. The dinners
are all the same and the 'host' invariably makes you drink a glass of
sherry and bitters to improve your appetite. Their dinners are the
only thing they do well, and they are tremendous feeders and always
drink champagne and hock etc. at these Sunday orgies, so you see we
live like fighting cocks.

When George writes from Ingestre in 1864 he gives a more pleasing
picture – that of beautiful Lady Adelaide Talbot, his cousin, afterwards
Lady Brownlow, decorating the house for Christmas:

> Dear Papa
>   Yesterday I rode on the Chase with Alice [Kerr] and Adelaide,
> then went out shooting, and then helped to decorate the house – I
> was stuck on a pair of steps on the sideboard to put wreaths on the
> tops of the pictures. Adelaide was too lazy when asked to help, said
> she had quite enough to do to drink her tea …

Gussy was the model son; he worked at school, won prizes and
never complained or asked for money. Grandpapa's thoughts followed
him lovingly when he went to Ceylon as a tea planter in 1873.

Letters began to reach Withington describing Ceylon and its
coasts, its palms, its spicy breezes. He is interested in home news, in
the Colesbourne shooting, the visits Adela and Emma are paying and
in the fortunes of Withington village, and he evidently pictures the grey
cottages, the wandering stream of the Coln and the coverts, as he sits in
his veranda with his dogs or jogs round the plantations on his pony.

Gussy regularly replies to the mails from home. He is doing well and will soon be home on leave. Later he is to fall in love with Susan Elwes, his cousin, and take her back to Ceylon as his wife. She too enjoyed the flowers and the ponies and the native dresses, and other planters found her a gay hostess, very English and unspoilt.

Next in order comes, to me, the person most interesting in the family, Emma, my mother's favourite and much loved sister, who helped to form her tastes, and whose ill health and early death gave a tragic tone to the Withington household. All this left a picture sharply etched upon the younger sister's imagination, which later became imprinted on my own mind.

I was called 'Emma' as a second name. Her Bible was given to me at nine years old, and now, as I read the letters and diaries and recollect all my mother told me of her, Emma lives before my eyes. She was tall, had a rounded, oval face and slanting eyes, a high forehead and nose 'legerement retroussé'. Lively and impulsive, she yet had the power of applying herself to those subjects, like music, which she wished to learn; she was sympathetic, especially to children, and a great lover of society. In spite of the consumptive condition which gave her existence many ups and owns, perhaps partly because of it, her life was both full and vivid. A childish letter in 1861 tells how the children went from Colesbourne to Cirencester, and enjoyed a country peepshow:

> My dear Mama,
>   I went to the dancing yesterday at Cirencester, there was such a mop, we saw it out of the windows, there was such a crowd that we could not go out at all, we had some lunch at the King's Head, and called our tea when we got home, a late dinner, as we had sausages and a Damson tart which was very good indeed. There was a theatre in the Market Place and pictures of the fall of Delhi, and the great fire in London, and the Royal Family, and Prince Alfred [*sic*] looked horrid, they all had light hair,
>   With best love, I am ever your most affect. daughter
>   Emma Frances Talbot

Then Emma's diary, reminding one of the 'Ministering Children' and of the naïve woodcuts in children's books, describes her life at 14, the stock figures of nursery legend, the poor widow, the pony, the Mademoiselle, the Aunts, duly appearing in its pages:

July 1866
Adela cross because she could not gather roses. Played the organ ...
dried flowers and pasted them. Fine, sunny ... went to see Mrs Cork,
went to Mrs Laight and Mrs Williams... went out riding, Mlle. Roy
walked with me. Played the organ for an hour. Changed my habit
and took the rest of our pudding to Mrs Cork with Mlle. ... went by
fields and home by the village. Evening pasted flowers ... sore throat,
cold ...

19th Friday
Played the organ at 3p.m. as soon as had begun Papa and Mama
(who had been away) drove up in a fly ... I had not had the letter to
say they were coming, as Papa had not posted it, Edith, Evelyn, and
Johnny Elwes came in the basket and I could not go back to my dear
organ. They went at 4.15 and we took the half holiday, Mlle. drew the
inside of the church. Went out riding 9.30 ... to old Sarah Becher's,
the pony fell down and cut its knees, made things for the school feast
... gathered roses, fine.

11th August
Adela's birthday was kept ... school feast ... went out before breakfast
and made her a bouquet ... Mlle. Roy made her a wreath ... morning,
made wreaths to decorate the school house ... afternoon, changed
my frock ... Johnny and Mlle. Berger came. They had tea at 5, little
tea things.

25th Saturday, morning
Made 3 pots of cuttings ... after lunch drove to Colesbourne in
the basket with Guss ... Adela came in the spider with Papa ... Sir J.
Campbell gave me his photo ... Johnny was stung with the wasps,
Adela was with him and had her ears boxed ... Aunt Mary was very
angry. I was scolded because I was in the park looking at the cricket
when it happened.

In 1866 she was sent abroad for the winter and went on with her
studies, in Italy and France. At home, keeping up with all her cousins
and friends, contriving dresses, on a small allowance, travelling with a
maid, learning to play the church organ, 'poor peopling', writing letters,
gave her plenty of interest. Besides she kept a diary and, in later days,
in spite of often being 'very tired', the wonderful album had to be kept
up to date, with new photographs of young men, young ladies in ivy
arbours and children on velvet chairs, around which the delicate flowers
and leaves had to be painted. The albums are works of art, but, for me

at least, it is in the letters that Emma has unconsciously drawn her own portrait with point and delicacy, so I let them go on telling their story. Straight from the careful education of the Withington schoolroom and the French governesses, Emma writes letters that are surprisingly mature for 14 years.

They relate mostly to people, lessons and flowers – she is sure of an interested response at home. She learns carving at Cannes, where she is staying with her aunt and uncle, Lady Emma and Colonel Patrick Talbot:

> Gave Aunt Emmie a hand-looking glass of which I had carved the frame in ivy leaves.
>
> Last night the Buccleughs [*sic*] arrived, Uncle Pat went to meet them at the station, and they will probably come here between churches, as they have luncheon with Lord Henry, who lives close to this house, their house being about three miles out in the country, which just suits them, the Duke wanting a rest and to be out of society; the two girls, Lady Mary and Lady Margaret, are in the schoolroom still.
>
> From Florence in 1866 Emma writes to Gussy:
>
> We went to the Pitti with Papa, so went through it rather too quickly, but Uncle Edmund showed me all the best things at the Uffizi. The two pictures that charmed me above everything are the 'Samian Sybil' and the 'Angel of the Annunciation', the former by Guercino and the latter by Carlo Dolci. Also a beautiful one by Raphael, 'St John preaching in the wilderness'.

Her favourite pictures are of the late Italian school, the fashion of the period. Primitives were not admired until later. But a Pre-Raphaelite comes on the scene as well, Holman Hunt on one of his journeys, backwards and forwards to Palestine, is staying in Rome: 'There is a Mr Holman Hunt here, he has lodgings over us and is a great artist, he dines with us every night. He painted "The Light of the World" and the "Presentation of the Temple", so it is something to know him, isn't it? I shall buy you a photograph of the Arch of Titus and a Roman scarf or two.'

Emma writes on her first journey abroad, when her father travelled with her:

November 1866

> Dearest Mama,
>
> We are not so tired as usual, as coming Vetturino is comparatively easy work as we sleep every night and get up at five which we think

nothing of now then breakfast is at five thirty then off at six, when it is nice and cool. About twelve we stop at a town on the way to rest the horses and as we keep along the sea-shore we go down onto the beach, generally we get to the town that we are going to stay all night at about 4.30 and then table d'hote (which I like very much), soon after we go to bed. Coming we saw such quantities of maiden-hair on the rocks by any little stream or any damp place. Papa pulled up a plant to take back but I do not know if it will live. Myrtles, Oleanders, Sweet Williams, Snapdragons, Roses etc., all grow wild on the mountains, the myrtle is *much* larger than ours and so sweet ... the hotels at Nice and Paris were free from insects but at San Remo and Finale there were plenty ... I was looking through the visitors book and I saw 'R. Talbot, London'. Papa says it is Reggie. The people work just the same on Sunday and all the shops are open and everything the same only you see all the women with a white scarf over their heads and shoulders. The best dressed have muslin ones ... I was rather disappointed in the towns, the streets are so narrow and so dirty and they smell.

Emma enjoys the pictures and frescoes and Uncle Edmund seems a good cicerone:

Rome, 17 November 1866

Dearest Mama,

We arrived here about 11 o'clock Thursday evening. We left Florence at 5 a.m. Tuesday, and arrived at Ellora at 1 o'clock, we took a carriage and four horses to Perugia, where we slept. As soon as we got there we went out to see the sights of which there are plenty. First we saw a magnificent old palace and fountain, then we went into the cathedral and then we went back to the hotel and had dinner at table d'hote. We went to see some lovely frescoes in the Sala del Cambio by Perugino and to the University to see the pictures. In the afternoon we went to the Church of San Pietro, there are such quantities of pictures in it, and such a beautiful view from a gallery outside it was not a very clear day, but still it was delightful. Perugia is a very old town, with all the old fortifications, we did a great deal considering the short time that we stayed there. We arrived at Foligno at 1.30, we had an hour to wait. There was such a crowd, but I was not stared at quite so much as usual, though I came in for a good share of attention [an allusion to her height] ...

Everything was ready for us when we got here, tea and chickens; Aunt Lucy hardly thought that the people of the house would be up but they were, and all was quite comfortable. I like Rome so much and yesterday morning we went out and ordered a pair of thick boots for me, as my old ones quite struck work after the journey and my new ones are rather tight. Aunt Lucy likes my things very much, and we are going to have something done to my old hat, as this journey has quite put an end to it. I am very much obliged for your long letter, which I received this morning before the expedition to Rome. I am very glad that Adela is better and that you went to Colesbourne, as you would have been so dull alone. On Monday I am to see Dr Topham, and I will write after to tell you what he says. I am quite well now, and it is so warm here after England.

Believe me ever, Your most loving daughter,

Emma Frances Talbot

Emma describes the people she meets in Rome:

Aunt L. wishes me to tell you that her party consist of old maids, as she has Miss O'Brien, Lord Inchiquin's sister, Miss Forbes, Miss Hosmer, a delightful little Yankee sculptress, rather a lion here, who dresses in the most absurd way; when we go to her studio, there she is, with her grey hair quite short and curly, and funny little man's face with a velvet sculptor's cap on, and a velveteen jacket, just like a man's hunting coat; but to return to the old maids, Miss Cushman and the two Miss Dempsters, who are not old maids, but always talk of themselves as 'sich'. I have been obliged to give Miss Dempster the photo of myself that I had for Aunt L. and as I am always being asked for my photo: I had better be done again while I am here.

Mama has asked what the food is like:

You asked what food we get, it is very good; in Rome people have their dinners and luncheons in a trattoria, and we have soup for the servants, one dish of meat and one of vegetable in the middle of the day which is our luncheon (with the help of buns, cake, bread and jam, and Devonshire cream), and the servants 'diner': soup two dishes of meat and of vegetables, and a pudding in the evening at seven, for our dinner and the servants supper. We have had green peas, and asparagus and plenty of young artichokes cut in half and stewed with some sauce but the *choke* is all there so that you can eat them, leaves and all barring the outside, which requires more chewing to get down safely. How enterprising of Aunt Emma to build a house at Cannes, if I have to leave England next year she had better take me as nursery governess. Monday was 'Festa' when it is abominable as the shops are shut and it is impossible to get a carriage, and every out of the way place filled with people, so, as it was Grotto Ferrata fair which is supposed to be a very pretty sight, Uncle E. thought he would go with a friend of his to Frascati by the 7.30 and walk to Grotto Ferrata about two miles further and come back to Frascati after the fair.

Emma is ardent and painstaking in the pursuit of culture:

> Rome 18 December 1866.
>
> Dearest Papa and Mama,
>
> I wish you both a merry Christmas and a happy New Year, this is the second Xmas I have been away from home, and I hope that next year I shall not be away ... tell Gussy to write soon, and tell me all about the ponies and his drawings etc; as Aunt Lucy wants to know what he does and what is his best point, and if he likes trees, animals or people best. She has made a quantity of very pretty sketches, and she says she will lend some to Gussy to copy when she gets back to England. I have only one singing lesson this week as, if I practice that is quite enough, I am getting on a little now, I cannot sing higher than E. Practising before breakfast does not tire me, as I have a cup of coffee and some bread and butter before I am dressed. I have not had my chest painted again as Doctor Topham says that it is not ready yet as it is not worse and is rather better which is a good thing ... Uncle Edmund reads 'Roba di Roma' to us in the evening; what a charming book it is! you read it last summer did not you!
>
> It does not seem as if Gussy would be eighteen the day that you get this. Give him my best love, and tell him that I wish him many very happy returns of the day, and I hope he will have a real *moustache* when next I see him. Yesterday it rained in the morning and as I could not go out, I made myself a collar, I thought it would be much more difficult; but Martin only cut it out and I made it and finished it, one row of plain stitching and another in that coarse crotchet cotton and a little sprig in Point à la Minute in each corner, that I invented, and that Aunt Lucy says is very pretty; I was quite charmed by my first experience in collar-making. I remembered what you told me about doing things by halves and tried to make the corners sharp etc ...

Emma writes to Gussy about everything she can think of that will interest him in Rome:

Rome, 26 December 1866

Dearest Goose,

Thank you very much for your letter it was very good of you to write to me during the exams as you must have been very busy; but the effort was fully appreciated. I thought of you on the 24th and we drank your health. You want me to buy you photos, how much do you mean to spend? How big do you want them and are they to be of the popular ruins such as the Forum, the Arch of Titus, and Severus, and the Temple of Vesta. Apropos to that if you want a pretty ink-stand you can get one for 5 or 6 francs in the shape of the Temple of Vesta, round, with columns all round, or the tomb of Cecilia Metella which is not so pretty. Please answer all these questions ... yesterday morning I went to St Peter's with Martin, and Robert to take care of us and to get a carriage for us, to hear the far-famed silver trumpets that are only played twice a year at Xmas and Easter and to see the Pope carried down the church. I picked up three gentlemen to take care of me, Mr Barrett, Mr Cavendish Taylor, and Mr Edwards so I was quite safe. The whole thing was very impressive and grand. The two rows of soldiers down from the high altar to the door, the Swiss Guard in their yellow, red, and black striped dress with their armour on. The Guardia Nobile in their scarlet coats; the members of the household in their black satin gowns and white ruffs round their necks, the cardinals in their scarlet robes. The Monsignori in their purple ones and all the different soldiers mixed among the crowd made a very gay sight; then the Pope carried down on his chair with his three triple crowns borne before and the Greek and Armenian prelates in their rich gold and silver robes and the cardinals preceding him and his two great fans of light ostrich feathers on each side of him, all put together was a sight too soon over and that you hardly think is real after it is gone and you wish to see it again that you may remark every little detail; as the Pope passes blessing the people the soldiers and all the crowd fall on their knees. The Zouaves are so very much disliked that everyone thinks there will be a revolution during the carnival. Their dress is very picturesque, a short round jacket of grey cloth trimmed with scarlet braid, a scarlet sash round their waists, and *very* loose sort of knickerbockers, and white gaiters; they wear no collars and their jackets are cut low at the neck; three of them have been killed, two by the people who hate them as they must all mercenary troops and say that if they do not go they will send the poor old Pope away which would be a *great* shame.

Goodbye Sir and please write to me again when you have time, an article very hard to find in Rome. Believe me, Ever you very affectionate sister,

Emma Frances Talbot

Emma at 15 writes to Adela who was nine: 'I am glad you are getting on with your music, if you take my advice you will spare no pains for you will be quite repaid after'. The 15-year-old mentor goes on in another letter to her mother: 'I have read *The Days of Bruce* and should not have thought it at all the book for Adela, being nothing more than a novel, only it is historical, but I suppose it will not do her any harm to read it.'

In 1867 11-year-old Adela gets a letter about Roman society, with some sententious remarks about how to behave from Emma:

I shall soon be home now; I shall have such a quantity of little tales to tell you about what I do. The people here and the compliments that I get, the people innocently thinking that I am grown up, and I do not undeceive them (at least not the men) but answer most properly. I never thought that I should be able to do so, but when the time comes the answers come and I have the credit of being witty, which is a great nonsense as here if one says the stupidest thing without thinking one is supposed to be witty. There is a horrid little man, a Yankee, who is so stupid and who says such stupid things and everybody impresses on me, or rather tries to do so, that he is very clever; if I were to say half the things that I think I should be thought so too, but I always try to consider before I say them, if they are unkind or silly or forward, so I do not get into a muddle by saying wrong things to the wrong person, simply because I think before I speak; as all *little* girls should do. This will not amuse you much, but, *how-some-dever* when I come home we will have fun and talk, and chatter, and laugh, and sing, and everything else *improper*. Aunt Lucy says that I will find Withington dull after all the parties here, but I never shall find *home* dull, it is quite a different affair when I go home, I shall fall into home ways, I shall not wonder who will call, or if anyone will take us out driving, or who I shall meet out walking, or at a party, and I shall not expect to be asked out in the evening, or to be talked to and asked to dance beforehand at a ball I am not going to ...

She is anxious to bring home some presents:

Now you naughty child, the next time that you write if you will not tell me seriously mind you, and solemnly what I am to get, I will not bring you anything; should you like a sash, a Roman collar ... or an ornament of any kind as models of the columns of the Forum in bronze, now answer me do you hear?

E.F. Talbot

(This stern moralist is 16 and she writing to Adela who is 11 years old). The question of clothes comes up again:

Rome, 16 February 1867

My old grey gown has struck work, and as my Lindsey is getting too hot, I am very sorry to say that I am obliged to have a new gown, but as I wanted a skirt, I am going to have one of white alpaca, braided in black (which will be my work) and a skirt of some sort; I shall wear it first on Sundays to save my blue, and when it has to do weekdays, I shall wear my old llama skirt, instead of the new one, and make that do Sundays and 'Festas' with my blue skirt. On Thursday we went to meet with Miss O'Brien (the correct thing here) it was at Monte Mario, and the view was lovely, past all descriptions, and the views over the Cornice were lovely but a different kind of thing, more bare rugged rocks, here the Alban hills are so soft and blue and the Sabine hills more rugged; when I get home I shall read Roman history with much more pleasure than I ever did before. The Arbuthnots promised to take us to the Opera the same night which I was looking forward to with immense delight, but the day was one of disappointment, as we were finishing dinner in walked old Sir Robert, to say that they had heard that there was to be a great fuss, bombs thrown etc., as all the Cardinals would be out at the Spanish Ambassador's reception which was that night, and he did not think it would be safe; but we were to come and spend the evening with them which we did and enjoyed ourselves very much; they are going to take us next Wednesday and we hope that it will be *Tosso* the best Opera here, and if so we shall be the gainers as it would have been *Macbeth*, in which the best singers do not sing. I went to St Peter's on Sunday. It was not the St that was to be canonised the other day, but another that died a very long time ago, as they have to wait 100 years I think before they are canonised after their death. Some people say that it was to please the people and give them something to think about; Rome is not as quiet as it was.

Yesterday the troops were being marched about the town to frighten the people as the day before there had been a few squabbles and a little fighting; and last Sunday we were told that at the Bridge of S. Angelo there was fighting between the priests, Sbirri and Zouaves...

I have nothing more to tell you except that when the Italians get into passion they are in such a fury that they take *castor oil* after, I am not trying to impose upon you, but it is quite true, coming home from the meet we met a man whose horse had cast a shoe, he was an Italian and his face was red with rage, he was trotting his horse all down Monte Mario on the hard road and its hoof was broken all in a fringe. Aunt Lucy and I thought he would want a great deal of castor oil; I saw him yesterday and his face was quite a different colour, Aunt Lucy wishes me to say that she things the remedy must have the proper effect.

Emma is enjoying the company but thinks longingly of Withington:

Aunt L. and Uncle E. have engagements for every day this week, on Monday evening Uncle E. dined out, Tuesday Miss Greathed and Mr Barret dined and went on with us to the Arbuthnots', who live so close and always make such a point of my going that I generally do, last night to a dance at Miss Greathed's who also lives close by, I enjoyed it very much, I wore my grenadine and forget-me-nots in my hair, we came home at 1 a.m. so if my letter is stupid its because I am rather tired. I do not *always* go out so much and a great many invitations have been refused, but this dance was an exception to the rule of 'not going out'. I had to order a pair of white satin shoes for it. ... We saw in 'Galingani' that Aunt Mary has a son, so I now possess 43 first cousins ...

I am very glad that Gussy had such a good day's hunting, they hunt a good deal here, in the Campagna, but we have not been to the meet, most of the young ladies hunt, and I believe it is rather dangerous work, with all the ruins about. I was very amused at Papa telling the farmer about our journey; I suppose that I shall be 'quite a strainger' when I come home, I hope that poor old Mrs Cork is better and that she will live till I return; I am looking forward to seeing you all again, not that I am not happy here, for I like Rome *very* very much, but, I should enjoy it more if you could see it too.

To share the sights of Roma and the flowers with 'Mama' and the family is the one thing lacking:

Rome, 22 March 1867

My Dearest Mama,

Thank you very much for your last letter which I received on Monday, you say that your letters are not amusing, but allow me to contradict you, I like hearing everything, all the 'picole cose' as we call them. ... How I pity you, what weather you have endured, if you could be transported suddenly on to the Pincio you would think that you *were* in Italy and no mistake, in the first place you would find it rather too hot to walk about and the sun rather bright in your eyes, accustomed as they are to snowdrifts, but when you had taken a seat on one of the benches or little iron chairs and looked about you will feel better, the orange trees in blossom, the China roses and Banksia roses too all out, the Judas trees and rhododendrons in full flower beside several other plants and shrubs whose names I do not know; then three or four fountains in the middle, and a great palm tree in the centre of the space where the band plays, oh! It is charming the whole place smells of firs and the birds sing most delightfully; the mountains too on one side so dim and hazy, and St Peter's in front, looking so hot, as the sun bakes down upon it; the cyclamen are out in the Borgheses and lovely they are; we hope to find a great many in the Vatican Gardens today.

And in 1867 she writes of the music master at Cannes, who is displeasing to her in some of his habits:

Monsieur Laussel, is not good looking, very brusque and makes very low bows. My music lesson is over, he is so particular but I am very glad as I have a chance of playing well, he will not spoil me with praise ... he has some horrid kind of pomatum and *smokes*. A day or two ago I coughed up a little blood but it is nothing to be alarmed about ... there is no chance of getting into the new house before Saturday ... and there is to be an orange grove with walks about it, doesn't it sound romantic? The horses are to come, two little grey Arabs ... as to work, I have braided myself a band to match my Zouave jacket, it looks very well, I am going to put the lace on the muslin apron, on to the black silk one, and there will be enough trimming ... to trim a muslin garibaldi ... Mr B – is very good natured, he is not of the highest order of society and talks through his nose. We also learn that Aunt Emma is not shocked at people reading story books on Sunday.

Cannes, 1868

I have got so tired of my music, but Ralph (Kerr) have me a spur, he told me I had plenty of talent but not enough perseverance and he thinks I was born with a lump of cotton wool at the end of all my fingers. Aunt Cecil will certainly not be home when I am as they got to Mentone today and stay there and at San Remo and Rome for some time.

In 1868 she describes a picnic in high society. If the picture reminds one of Edward Lear's rhymes and drawings it is perhaps not accidental. Lear spent much time at Cannes and was a friend of Lady Emma Talbot.

> Last Saturday I went on an excursion with the H. Scotts, Mr Vesey, Lady Wharncliffe, Mrs Swinton, Mr Ryder, His Grace [The Duke of Buccleuch] and Mary and Margaret. Lady H and myself, being non-walkers, went on donkeys. The rest of the party walked, except Lady W. and Mrs S. who went in carriages with the luncheon, round by the road, while we went across the mountains, it was such fun. I broke my parasol across my donkey's back, much to the Duke's amusement, the Duchess has promised to get me a new one. We had luncheon out of doors on the rocks, and a most lovely view of Nice and the Cornice, we all took a short walk and I got some plants of fern, and went back in the carriages.

At 17 Emma sometimes finds her elders rather boring:

> Last night a few people came to dinner, all old formalities, dear me, how fearfully dull the evening was, on Saturday Lord Mount Edgcumbe and Lord Saint Asaph, the Duke and Levetts I think dined here, today the Duke, and I think Mr Vesey, come to luncheon and go out rowing with Uncle Pat and Lord Mount Edgcumbe, after I go to a concert with Mrs Swinton ... Mr Spinablli made me a very pretty speech on Tuesday, he said if I got on so fast I should soon not want any lessons, he has found a talent for composition in me, what a bore the people are, always finding out talents because then it is on my conscience if I do not cultivate them, and really I have no time in this fine weather for I ought to be out all day. On Monday Lady Henry Scott came to luncheon and to sing with Aunt Emmy. Argent has made my skirt with the embroidery I made and it is so pretty, she is now making my old blue muslin tidy, I am sure that a good maid is an immense saving, take my old brown linsey for example, and my muslin will be so pretty, the blue ribbon that was bought to do up my white grenadine is to be split in half as it is too wide and ruched to trim the body, the skirt is gored.

(Emma is still the frugal child of the parsonage.) Back again in Rome, evidently longing for someone from home to share the sights with her, she writes: 'It is so fine and warm and charming and delightful, I only wish you could come and see and judge for yourself whether it is not better than "Some place in England with the help of a horse and a respirator" (which someone had evidently recommended).'

Emma's descriptive letters, with the Roman villa gardens with their tiny cold-pink cyclamen and harlequin red and white camellias, the Zouave jackets, the hunting amid the 'dangerous ruins' of the Campagna, show the formal bariole life of the English colony in the '60s who all live near one another in the neighbourhood of the Via de Capo le Case. She talks like 'an old young lady' at 15, learns singing from Mustafa, the middle-aged castrato soprano of St Peter's, and goes to the great church to hear him sing his arias. The three triple crowns precede the Pope down the vast aisle of St Peter's at the ceremony of the funeral of the two cardinals.

She sits in the Vatican Gardens, while Aunt Lucy sketches in water-colour, no doubt laying on cobalt to imitate the clear blue of the sky overhead. Her descriptions of scenery and of the flowers are pleasant. The English people interest her more, however, and the remarks they make about herself most of all.

> 68 Via Di Capo le Case, Rome, 24 January 1867
>
> Dearest Mama,
>
> Thank you very much indeed for you two last letters the first of which dated January 13th I received on the 19th and the other from Brockhampton, on the 23rd yesterday. I do not envy you the English climate at present; here, when it freezes in England, it either rains or is beautifully fine, as it was yesterday, with a deep blue sky overhead and the sun so bright and warm. I truly wish that *all* of you could come over and enjoy it with me, and then my enjoyment would be complete. Yesterday we went out driving into the Campagna and the mountains were a lovely soft purple against the clear blue of the Italian sky and the Convent on Monte Cavo stood out quite white; the different villages Tivoli, Frascati, Grotto Ferata, Rocca di Papa etc., look so pretty on the sides of the mountains. The Master of Lovat says that I have not done growing, which is very kind of him but I do not appreciate the compliment ... you would be amused if you saw me at the parties, as a grown-up young lady, I play my part very well, and at first I used to be in such a fright, but now I am used to it and keep them all going if there are any stupid ones and Aunt L. cannot *do* them all at once ...
>
> The violets and anemones are just coming out in the Borghese gardens, they do not grow in the hedges as in England, but in the turf, and in the Spring it is covered with them. A Roman has stabbed

a Zouave and is going to be shot in the Piazza del Popolo at the north end of the boiso, I only hope that we shall not see it for we do not know what day it takes place and from the Pincian you look straight down on to the Piazza and go through it on the way to our church which is outside the gates of the town.

In the Spring, before returning to England and to Withington, Emma protests that she will 'not be dull'. One feels that her contented nature and pluck account for her popularity. The summers are passed in visiting Alton and Ingestre and Lord Bagot's at Blithwood, where cricket matches are in full swing. The young gentlemen engage her attention, though she understands 'nothing of the game'.

> Alton Towers, 8 August 1871
>
> When I was getting into the train, Lord Henry Paget appeared and came with me to Alton, he was very good-natured and pointed out all the places along the line, but rather dull ... I wore my little ivy and pearls last night, it was very pretty. I am in charge today and the people keep on bothering to know what I am going to do and when I am thinking of going to the cricket which makes me *very* shy. I must finish this in a hurry as we are off almost immediately to the cricket. It was quite charming there this morning; we may have a tent to ourselves and *comfortable* chairs.

Emma is resourceful about dress:

> You may like to hear about my 'colours' which everyone has been pleased to examine excessively. My winter hat that I travelled in is the victim, I took off the Sang-de-boeuf feathers and velvet and put Zingari ribbon round the hat, and a black feather and three small red ones (which I luckily brought with me) and two bows of Z ribbon; it really is rather nice, but I can't wear it with my pink muslin so I must give up one or the other tomorrow. We *drive* to and from the cricket ground which is just behind the stables. The Gerald family have appeared, Aunt M. with a yellow bonnet and a *red* rose, and Maggie in mauve muslin and a bonnet.

At Withington Emma takes her place as dispenser of soup to the Poor People, like her mother before her, and Adela after her. If villagers were better off than they had been, they were still far from despising help from the gentry, which was given in a dutiful if friendly way, and not on any equalitarian basis but rather on that of 'let him that hath, minister to him that hath not'.

If Emma enjoyed the 'beau monde', she was a conscientious parson's daughter at Withington, as her letter in October 1871 shows; there is prophetic irony in the 'funeral hymn, ready in case of emergency', for she died four years later:

> 1871, Withington
>
> Dearest Mama,
>
> Will you write and say whether you want your purple rep sent? I have put down the butter and candles etc. as usual. Who is to have soup on Friday? Thomas Barnfield and Sarah Curtis are to have it today.
>
> We practised after service yesterday – we finished the Te Deum and learnt the funeral hymn, it is ready now in case of emergency! I caught a cold on Friday singing an hour in that cold church, but it will soon be well and won't prevent my going to Colesbourne.

The summers of 1870 and 1871 Emma was in England. She had a patch of gaiety when she spent the London Season in Curzon Street with old Miss Jane Talbot of Temple Guiting. Her letters to Adela describe a Victorian young lady's life during the Season. With a little jog to the imagination one can see as, one reads them, the dusty sunny streets, the carriages rolling along, parasols in evidence, crossing sweepers, cabs and beggars. Crinolines are giving way to bustles, waists are more defined. The Princess of Wales is acknowledged queen of fashion; the tiny bonnets she wears are affected by ladies in general.

Among the members of Emma's circle there is give and take, though a critical faculty in her is fostered by her position as a poor relation, and by her state of health. During these 'seasons', however, Emma seems to forget the financial troubles and ill health and to enjoy herself. I like to fancy the breathless interest of Adela, who was 16, receiving Emma's letters almost daily at Withington, finding the envelope each morning on the breakfast table, and sharing vicariously in Emma's personal and dressmaking triumphs. All June and July the letters came, with descriptions of the balls, the partners who smiled at her in the park, the Shrewsbury children, concerts at the Floral Hall, Ascot, church at St George's Hanover Square – no doubt Adela longed for gaieties herself. She would read them on the steps, with the smell of jasmine coming faintly from the wall – and no doubt the jasmine my mother kept in later years in a vase on her writing table in summer reminded her of those poignant letters, and the thrilling echoes of London life.

On a summer's evening, Adela walking and thinking of Emma in London would hear the ring doves coo in the trees and the musical call notes of plovers out in the open fields; and would walk home in the evening light and the clean washed turquoise sky over the bare green Cotswold hillsides. 'I suppose I shall come home some time next week. I shall be very glad, as this is rather an uncomfortable life, between Jane and William, and when I do go out I never see anyone amusing hardly ...'. Emma writes about shopping in the leisurely autocratic manner of the age:

> 25 Curzon Street, 1870
>
> I drove to Russell and Allenby's, did not get out, but told them to send black silk jackets and white ball gowns to look at ... Aunt F. wished me to tell Papa that the chestnut horse is worrying her life out, as since he has been in London he won't eat, and he is so thing that his ribs show ... This morning Lewis and Allenby sent a cart full of ball gowns and a young man and another cart full of jackets and a young lady. I chose a very pretty tarlatan white gown, trimmed all over with narrow flounces and ruches. I am going to Lady P.'s ball tomorrow night, as it is to be one of the very best this season, very few young ladies and 'all the men'.

One letter is about Emma's illness, and is interesting as showing how tuberculosis was treated in 1870, very differently from today:

> 25 Curzon Street, 8 June (1870 or 1871)
>
> My Dearest Mama,
>
> You remember my complaining of my leg I told Theresa who thought the best thing to do was to see a good man at once, so accordingly she sent for Prescott Hewitt who saw me this afternoon at Claridges'. Theresa was so kind, I saw him in her room: he says there is not another abscess forming and that he can stop it, but he thinks that it is nothing more serious and can put it right: he says that it is nothing whatever to do with my chest ... he said I was quite right not to ride ... I may dance, but be very careful to avoid a blow: this is good news to *me*. I had tea with Theresa and then drove with her and the children, we went through the park and swaggered up Constitution Hill and through the Horse Guards, though we saw no one to admire us. I saw Lady Ailesbury, who kissed her hand and grinned ...

As consumptives often are, Emma was lively:

> Curzon Street, 11 June 1871
>
> Dearest Mama,
>
> I am going to begin my letter now and get some of it written.

The concert at the Floral Hall was too charming. Patti sang six times, as she answered her three encores. She first sang 'The Last Rose of Summer', and 'Comin' thro' the Rye' as a second song. Then she sang a duet out of the *Stabat Mater* with Pauline Lucca which they repeated, and the last thing she sang was the shadow song from *Demorah*, she has such an execution and the number of shakes, one after the other, sounded like a bird. For that encore she sang the Scotch song ending each verse with 'I cannot, cannot, willnot, willnot, willnot, mussnot ...' and she sang it so well and the audience laughed out loud. Uncle J.H., Evelyn and Concy were there and seemed glad to see me, I am to go there to luncheon today. It poured with rain while the concert was on. As soon as we got back Emily came for me and we went to Mrs Dynedoch-Gardner's, where we saw all the Cumberland Place Legges and the Portman Square Elwes: the later amiable to a degree. There was music going on and a Mrs Ward sang beautifully. The Legges asked after you and they brought me back here. The Lutleys came for me again at 11 and we went to Mrs Fullerton's musical party; I wore my pink foulard and Emily her apricot and blue gown; she looked very well. I believe I am going to Mrs Cavendish Bentinck's ball tonight, but Theresa has not heard from her yet. Emily offered to take me to Mrs Heming's musical tea tomorrow afternoon, but I want to drive with Theresa, as I can't on Wednesday ... Theresa goes to Alton next week for a few days, for the Yeomanry review, from Monday till Thursday I think. I shall wear my yellow gown tonight if I go to the ball; Presley has done it up very prettily: yellow is more worn than any other colour, bonnets, gowns, and everything of it.

One gets very confused with so many parties. This letter has advice for Mama!

25 Curzon Street, 13 June 1870

Dear Mama,

I am so glad that you are coming up to London ... you can get rid of the objectionable steels in your crinoline, if you leave some behind for the bustle ... at quarter to five I shall start out in the brougham again to go and fetch the children [Talbot] from their dancing, and we are going out shopping together and I shall spend the evening with them ... it is so nice their being in London. Charlie [Shrewsbury] has lent the Lutleys his box at Ascot, for tomorrow, and has told them to take me and 'a man', it will be such fun; all my friends will be there, 1st Life Guards included, as Mr Dansey is going to drive down the coach, and it is popularly supposed that he will ask us to luncheon.

Emily has been introduced to him and he said he should have known her for my sister anywhere: Theresa says that I must wear my blue llama which I wore first yesterday and she admired excessively.

London Society and the prospect of Ascot seem to raise Emma's spirits:

Jane is not at all well, green gooseberries have disagreed with her, and she has seen Sir W. Jenner, who ordered her out of town for a few days, so at last we have settled that she is to go to Brighton tomorrow. I have three more balls ... I was very lucky to get to Lady E. Heneage's as a great deal of offence has been given by there only being five young ladies there, of which I was one and delightful I found it. Aunt Mary has asked me to a 'drum' on the 23rd. I suppose I shall have to go.

Emma goes to stay with Lord and Lady Dartmouth and the Legge cousins and writes from Patshull in 1870:

The people in the house are Lady Montgomery and two pretty daughters, Mr Sackville, Mr Cameron Hampden and Capt. Ramsden, Mr Townshend Brooke, and Charlie Wynne Finch. Lady Dartmouth asked me to stay on as Papa wants me to come that day I said I would ... I shall not be early enough to stop in Cheltenham to do any shopping. Last night there was the great excitement of having our hair powdered, it was a grand success, mine was whiter than any of the others and I had it much larger than usual and pink ribbon among it and a little pink and white cap, it was just like the heads in the picture, we all tried to copy them and to dress accordingly and so you may imagine how odd we all looked. No one was told before, and they were much surprised when we all marched in together. After dinner we acted a little and altogether it was great fun. Have my photos come? If so will you send on by return of post. Best love to all ...

Her boy cousin Lord Ingestre, of 12, writes: 'Nellie has got two photos of Florrie Hastings who I do not think you know. Oh! Oh! She is so pretty you cannot think. What are you doing to amuse yourself, Emkins? Please write to me soon.'

25 Curzon Street, 5 July 1871

Dearest Mama,

Many thanks for sending all the lace it will be very helpful ... We went on to Mrs Villebois' 'at home'; I found a good many people I knew there: Francis and Miss Gordon, Lord Clonmel, Michael, etc.

I was so tired when we got back and thankful to go to bed. In the morning yesterday Muratori appeared, he was very pleasant and gave me a sort of lesson: he told me that I had more voice than he had ever heard, twice as much as at the concert and that when I was 21 I should have 'une voix *superbe*' and now it is 'une belle voix'. That is good hearing! He said that if Miss Rogers 'etait musicienne comme vous, elle serait une artiste avec une voix, mais elle ne comprend pas la mesure': he made me sing my old songs to hear the difference and said that it was 'un plaisir d'écouter'. I suppose it is having heard so much singing and good music lately that has taught me how to bring out the notes, for I was not aware of this wonderful change. We went to Jane's box for the *Trovatore*, it was charming, but not as nice as some operas: Gragrami's 'Il ballen' was delightful and was encored and of course Patti was nice, but poor Mario is sometimes so horribly out of tune, it was the last time he sings in it. I found to my extreme horror the next morning that I had brought back a bug with me, I had never seen one before, and was so horror-struck that it departed and is roaming at large in the house. What beasts they are! It is raining too much to go out and I am tired. We have sent for Muratori to come this afternoon to give me a lesson. What a day for your Farmington visit: the Lutleys and George have gone to Oakington for the day; they will have a charming drive in these fretting showers ...

A comfortable existence it seems to us who look back, with the measured trot of a pair of horses, the grooms holding the horse's heads, maids busily packing trunks for young ladies going to London or on visits, pairs of gloves being taken out of their tissue paper, and the worst of tragedies if the sash or right had glove be left behind! The young ladies sing in the evenings, the young men listen, the old men applaud. Emma is made to sing – one fancies her running upstairs all of a flutter to fetch her music, on the surge of a little wave of excitement, but more composed as she descended again. Her breath is sometimes rather short.

Pleasant days, happy hopeful times, when she meets again some of the young men whom she knew in London. But the tall delicate Emma has heart flutters and then disappointments. Mr So-and-so was 'off hand' and the 'chaffing' and the 'delightful valse' do not lead on to the tender declaration that the proud touchy Emma evidently hoped for ... Her ill health is often a topic in the letters, 'they all thought me looking much better'. But an early grave and not marriage was to be her fate. Her letters to 'Dearest Adela' still remain neatly packed in a small mahogany writing case. In the more staccato passages of an otherwise smoothly flowing measure, one feels the hopes, flutters and disappointments, which found their only expression in writing to her sister – one can read between the lines.

On account of her ill health, Emma spent winters in the Isle of Wight, at 'Eardiston Villa', or at Belinda House, Ventnor, sometimes with her mother, sometimes with Adela. In November 1875 my grandmother writes to Adela from Ventnor:

> Papa arrived last night about six o'clock, we did not expect him, for it was such a stormy day ... Emma is taking her drawing lesson and therefore cannot write by this early post, which she wishes to do. I am to thank you for your long letter and for all the things you sent, she will not have her black silk jacket (alas! she did not need it) till the spring, so it is of no consequence and she will write in a day or two. This is a beautiful morning, the sea as usual roaring close to our open window. There was great excitement here, just in front of our house last night, from 7 to 9 o'clock. There were eight immense casks of palm oil washed up by the waves, supposed to have been thrown over by some vessel or to have come from a wreck: numbers of men went into the sea as far as they could and hauled the casks out with ropes. The coastguard man took possession of them; there was a crowd of people watching it all. I went with Papa ... Em is most flourishing, she walked on Sunday for two hours.

At Ventnor Emma and Adela made the acquaintance of Mr and Mrs T.J. Thompson, the parents of Alice Meynell who was already writing poetry. Their Pre-Raphaelite culture puzzled the Miss Talbots a good deal and they were surprised and amused when Mrs Thompson, showing them a row of daffodils in a field, exclaimed, 'We think this is a very Dantesque meadow.' This was not the way they were accustomed to hear daffodils described! They also made friends with the Mackworth Dolbens, the mother and sister of the young poet, who was connected with the High Church Movement and was the friend of Gerard Manly Hopkins. These literary people evidently found the two sisters touching and interesting.

Adela writing from Ventnor to her mother describes the life at the seaside with her invalid sister:

> Belinda House, 5 May
> On Sat we went to Alum Bay with the Shaw faction. We had a very comfortable waggonette and a capital pair of greys, who did the 24

miles to Alum Bay in less than three hours and a half. We started at
9.20. It was a very good day and the wind was not cold, tho' very strong
at Freshwater and Alum Bay. We went down on to the sands directly
we got there and I devoured an immense quantity of sandwiches,
hard-boiled eggs, cold chicken, etc. which Mrs S. had brought with
her. It was delightfully warm on the sands. I was quite surprised to
see the different coloured sands did not grow in bottles. The cliffs are
entirely of sand and almost every cliff is a different colour. We started
back at 4.15 and got back at about 7.45. We had dinner, during which
Mrs Parke came in to see how we were and then we went to bed, not
so tired as one might have expected after driving 48 miles. We took
Mrs Shaw and the Hanburys to Trinity next morning. The wind was
so cold coming out that I don't wonder Emma caught cold. Lemare
(the famous organist) played a most wonderful voluntary coming out,
one of the old organ tunes, with great claps of thunder in the middle.
He did the thunder beautifully: it made one feel quite queer. Best love
to Papa. It is a most dismal day.

> Your loving child, Adela.

In August 1875 Lord Shrewsbury, her uncle, wrote from Alton
Towers, to Emma, evidently intending to cheer his invalid cousin:

My dear old Emma,
    I think you will like a line from me in the midst of our gaieties to
say how Mummy and I miss you and to tell you how Taddy [Adela]
has been admired. I think she has enjoyed herself, though I fear your
absence has taken off (as it has to me) some of the pleasure. We have
had cricket, polo, and a dance, and all sorts of fun but I will not spoil
the sport of narration, which Taddy will favour you with, when she
gets home. I cannot be too thankful that Theresa and I are alright
this year. It makes one sympathise with those who are suffering. God
bless you old girl.

> Your affte coz
> Shrewsbury.

The summer of 1875 was Emma's last. She writes from Withington to
Gussy in Ceylon, telling how, accompanied this time by Adela, she went
to London to see Dr Gull:

29 June

Dearest Gussy,
    Thanks so much for writing to me. I did not write the last time

as I was at Ashcroft and rather done up with my London exertions. I managed to get through it all wonderfully well, but the noise, heat and bustle were dreadful: luckily there were only two days of it: I saw so many people and enjoyed it on the whole; Charlie Shrewsbury was so kind, he sent carriages of all sorts to convey me about: Adela and I felt very grand driving about in their great barouche with the 'steppers'. I saw Gull twice and am not much the wiser: he says I have got paralysis, which affects my eyes – I can only just manage to read and write now and my left hand has got so powerless I can hardly feed myself. I don't know if I shall ever get better, I hope so, as paralysis does get cured with time and I can do nothing to amuse myself. Adela is a great help, she is so good about waiting on me ... I am knitting you a pair of blue silk socks, but I get on so slowly that I sometimes think they will never be done. This rain is bad for the dear hay!

> Ever your loving sister, Emma F. Talbot.

To amuse her Adela describes the wedding of their cousin 'Nelly' to Lord Castlereagh. They were famous later on in society as Lord and Lady Londonderry:

> 2 October 1875, Alton Towers, Cheadle
>
> Dearest Emma,
>
> The wedding went off most satisfactorily, and no one wept visibly except Florrie a little at the end ... We went into the breakfast (which was a stand-up in the dining hall) as we liked; Charlie B. [Lord Charles Beresford] took me in and we afterwards went down to the armoury where they cut the cake and made speeches for the benefit of a crowd of tenants etc.: we then marched back, and the Primate chose to take me: he is a good old thing. Lots of people have sent you their love, but I have not time to write more. Nelly's gown was satin and lace and a wreath of natural flowers: she looked lovely. More next time.
>
> Your loving Adela

Adela went to stay at Brockhampton for a ball in October 1875 but her letters describing it are not very cheerful, and I fancy her heart is with her sister in the Isle of Wight. At any rate they were together again in November and I have a pathetic letter in Adela's handwriting 'dictated by Emma'.

> My feet have not been cold for a long time, the letter which we supposed to be lost has never come, you have not told us anything about the kitten. How nice the primulas sound. How is the choir going? Best love to Papa and Mama.

My grandmother has written on it, 'dictated by Emma when she could not write: the last letter I had from her'.

Emma died on 31 December 1875, her parents and Adela were with her; in Adela's diary is the poignant entry 'came back without Emma, 3 January 1876 ...'

Emma had been my mother's favourite sister and principal companion. The records of Emma's doings form a connecting thread through the Withington chronicle. After her death Adela's life changed. My grandmother died soon after, and from that time Adela had to manage her father's house and the village activities alone. She was constantly invited on visits by relations who felt she led a lonely existence in Gloucestershire, and so spent a good deal of time in their houses, meeting members of the 'ruling caste', as it is called, belonging in one sense to their world, and yet, as a parson's daughter, not quite belonging to it. The cares upon her shoulders, her father, the village and the loss of her sister made her feel apart; but her enjoyment of society, the kindness of her various hosts, the admiration of her good looks made the invitations irresistible.

Adela moved on in her cycle of visits to cousins, meeting great figures at Belton, Ashridge, Wilton and Oxford. She made new friends, met new cousins like Margaret Talbot, wife of Reggie Talbot, and Alice Gaisford, daughter of Cecil Lady Lothian; and then there was a young lady, Miss Violet Lindsay, daughter of General Lindsay whom she used to visit in London, who was shortly to marry Lord Manners, eldest son of the Duke of Rutland. Adela crosses the path of the 'souls'. Margot Tennant goes to the Naval Review with the same party, Lady Ribblesdale is at Wilton and talks pleasantly with her.

Miss Mackworth Dolben, writing in 1876 about Emma's death, advises Adela about her life and the planning of these visits, and the letter might have come straight out of the pages of Miss Charlotte M. Yonge:

> It is a pleasure to me to think about Emma ... I am sure of one thing, that God will teach you and lead you in the way he sees best and make her memory a blessing to you for life, as you long that it should be, whatever may be the manner in which you are able to realise and feel. This does not matter so much as *doing*, and in that you told me in that former letter, of your victories over self in daily life, one seems to read the surest proof of the blessing ... Cannot you make a compromise about your visits by going, only not staying so long? It must be perplexing to know what is right to do, and I remember so well, how,

before I gave up all visits on my father's account, I used to feel the
difficulty. I suppose the pity is to stay away long enough to break up
home habits and make oneself not wanted, or to make oneself feel an
extra, and not dependable. This must, I think, be wrong in a daughter,
even if parents wish her to visiting a good deal ...

After my grandmother's death in November 1876, it was still harder
for Adela to decide how far she ought to go into the world, for now
she was the only companion for my grandfather at Withington. She
followed Miss Mackworth Dolben's advice and made a plan about her
visits, spending at least one week in every four with her father. Her diary
is a record of visits with lists of the people she met and with little except
the name to make it interesting. She had no album with flowers painted
round the photographs and ivy tendrils wreathing its pages. That had
been Emma's prerogative.

When, soon after Emma's death, Adela went to stay with her cousin
Edward Talbot at Keble College, Oxford, she entered a different world.
Edward and Lavinia Talbot, by the way in which they linked together
Church, State and family tradition gave a special character to Keble.
Both were young, 'human' and kind, and both securely placed in the
world. Adela to them was the handsome daughter of the old uncle at
Withington, fulfilling since the death of her sister and mother, a lonely
task cheerfully, and with little relief. 'Few people have a more difficult bit
of life to go through', writes Lavinia, and Adela now began a relationship
with them which continued throughout their lives.

Edward Talbot, first Warden of Keble at 27, was the second son of
the Hon. John Talbot, KC, a famous parliamentary lawyer, and the elder
brother to my grandfather; Lavinia was the daughter of Lord Lyttelton
of Hagley in Worcestershire.

Church life, always familiar and delightful to Adela, took on a new
aspect at Keble, where constant services were held in the Chapel, and
where 'great questions', like social reform, were considered and discussed
at all times. A new set of interests sprung up for her and, compared
with a Gloucestershire rectory existence, Keble must have been
enlivening. Oxford itself was stimulating, and the scholars, politicians
and undergraduates who came to the house were a source of some
excitement to the young country lady. 'Mr Curzon was so sorry to miss
you,' writes Lavinia in one of her letters, of the future Lord Curzon. Not
only Mr Curzon, but Lyttelton brothers, Balfours, Cecils, Gladstones,
and many others came or attended the chapel in the college. Though

Adela's discreet diary of the time reveals little feeling, the way in which she spoke of Keble in later times showed the enthusiasm the diary was not allowed to betray.

Life at Keble was orderly, and a robust hospitality put into practice that Christian teaching which often puzzled Adela in church, with its injunctions which seemed so seldom carried out. It was the time of the second flowering of the Tractarian Movement. At home Adela read the works of Toynbee and Booth which she had heard eagerly discussed at Keble, so that on her next visit she was able to put in her oar and quote in the right or the wrong place. The talk was different from that of the Gloucestershire neighbours and the other families of cousins. Worldly interests (very real to vivacious Lavinia Talbot) shared a place with intellectual and religious ones. Lavinia's secure grip on life in all its aspects had a calming and heartening effect on Adela, and the rival claims of 'goodness' and 'worldliness' were effectively disposed of in her racy but unmalicious talk.

The College chapels, with their fine organs and choirs singing the hymns and reverberating anthems, delighted her. All the Lytteltons, including Lavinia, were musical. Bob Lyttleton had married Edith Santley, daughter of Sir Charles Santley, who had a beautiful voice. Adela Talbot evidently enjoyed accompanying Edith Lyttelton on the organ of Keble College.

Her diary tells something of her days at Keble, the stiff knee which gave Edward Talbot his characteristic walk, of College Gardens and Oxford luminaries.

> Keble. 10 July. Edward came into the drawing room and was put on to the sofa, being moved on the stretcher ... Mr. Salter came with his canoe and took us up the river. Quite lovely and very hot. Mr and Mrs Hassell came to tea and we afterwards played tennis. Then the children blew for me while I played the organ in the Chapel. Afterwards with the children and Mr Moore to the Pusey Quad Garden. After dinner Edward read *The Faerie Queene* to us. I played.

> 11th ... Mrs W. Lyttelton came to dinner when the Warden was wheeled into the dining room. After he read *The Faerie Queene*, Mrs Bob sang; most lovely it was.

> 12th Sunday. Holy Communion in the Warden's room at 8, Mr Gore [Bishop Gore] officiating. Service at the Cathedral at 10. In the afternoon, Mrs Bob and I went with the children to the organ; she

> sang hymns while I played, then she read wonderfully at the sight as
> she played.

Keble, built of coloured brick in imitation of Italian marble, and other
Victorian brick houses of north Oxford, soon give way as one walks
towards the city, to the older streets with their character of an English
country town, interspersed with college buildings and churches: St
Giles', the Broad, with its unmistakable outline, and the strange figures
of broken grey stone in front of the Sheldonian. Here cabs rattled along,
foot passengers and errand boys jostled in the dust of the High. On the
river punts and boats slid along in ghostly quiet, shaking the reflections
of the willows in the water to the accompaniment of the dip of oars and
punt poles.

To recapture the religious atmosphere of a past day is as difficult
as to recall the smell of a flower bed. Victorian ideas may seem to us
something to admire, to regret, or to laugh at, but their value lies
in their having really existed and not so very long ago. The sermons
published in many volumes, that have no sale today, once vibrated
through vaulted ecclesiastical buildings, giving a thrill of warning or of
comfort, of intercommunication between preacher and congregation.
For eloquence was one of the joys of Victorian existence. No doubt the
17th-century English of the Authorised Version of the Bible gave the
rhythm, stiffened by 18th-century formality. Perhaps the 'magnificent
sermon' heard by my grandfather in Lichfield Cathedral was one of these.
Grandfather was content with driving his horses and never considered
preaching such a sermon himself.

The Evangelical revival (which influenced the Church of England)
suggested the value of reading the Bible and going to church regularly,
while the Tractarians, on the other hand, stressed the church's year, its
festivals, fasts and saints' days. It may not be amiss to remember that
Pusey and Keble, the early Tractarians, were both of good family and
accustomed to the regular life of big houses which made a system and
form seem natural and right. Arnold was a broad churchman. In his
sermons (1840) I find, 'I concluded my sermon last Sunday with dwelling
upon the necessity of everyman's being brought to say in earnest, "what
must I do to be saved"?' This strikes the note of religious life at that
time.

Salvation, according to the Evangelicals, was to be attained by
Inner Light and Guidance; Catholics and Tractarians stressed the

sacraments, confession and direction; while moderate churchmen held that sacraments and services are the means of grace through which good works, as laid down in the church catechism, and that individuals use or abuse this means. Leaders of religious thought like Liddon, Jowett, Liddell, and later Charles Gore, Henry Scott Holland and Edward Talbot, were men who could use them and who seemed able to deal with the world outside the church, because they knew a good deal about the lump that was to be leavened.

If the aristocratic tradition in England had much about it that was noble, its grandeur could overlay and oppress its own children. A purge was needed to keep this tradition healthy. Disraeli, a foreigner and a Jew, who saw magnificence becoming arrogant, privilege oppressive and refinement selfish, considered the Christian religion the cure for all these ills and he valued the Established Church.

In 1878 Adela had a letter from her cousin Adelaide Brownlow, in her interesting illegible handwriting, inviting her to stay at Belton in Lincolnshire:

> 4 Jan. 1878
>
> My dear Adela,
>   Gertrude tells me you have been to Wilton and it has just struck me that perhaps you might like to come here for a ball which we have promised to go to on Thursday next at Grantham? If Uncle Gustavus would let you come I should be so glad to know you a little. I don't think we have ever met since you were quite a little girl …

Adela went to Belton. Her first sight of the beautiful Wren house should have been something of an experience, but her diary notes only the time of her arrival. The classical architecture of Wren meant little to her. Ruskin and the Gothic were the fashion of the hour, and besides she still had to be awakened to the deeper aesthetic interests.

The charm of Belton lies in its classic formality. From a central hall with high windows one looks out on one side over a wide avenue of lime and elm trees to iron gates a great distance away, and on the other side over wide shallow steps to a formal garden. If the style is French, the flavour is decidedly English. The house was compact and comfortable. A staircase at either end of the house went up with easy steps to the floor above, containing the wide, light library, and to 'Lady Brownlow's boudoir' as it was called. A white daylight, of 18th-century clarity, flooded the rooms through the high windows. Orderly continuity reigned, marble busts stood in the hall, and fine gilt console tables, with supporting gilt greyhounds, stood where they had since the house was built in the reign of William and Mary. The portrait of Lord Chancellor Cust, with a roll in his hand, commanded the scene. In winter, massed sweet-smelling flowers recalled the great garden without. The chapel, grey-panelled, red-cushioned and stiff, brought back the reign of Queen Anne. Panelling in the chapel drawing room was painted like green malachite, Lely portraits with their curious 'stuffed' and unreal appearance hung on the walls. From the windows another avenue met the eye, sweeping up the hill to the left of the house to a 'folly' at the top. The bedrooms too were beautiful and sumptuous in the heavy style of the period. The blue brocade bedroom and dressing room had their grand canopied beds, the Chinese room had an 18th-century Chinese wallpaper, doors and mantelpieces were carved and painted, each bit of work exquisitely satisfying on the eye. In the small dining room were Cust family portraits, one by Hoppner of two brothers in black coats and white breeches fondling a dog, and a conversation piece containing many figures and a swing. The room looked on to the square entrance courtyard and the porte cochère with its clock, and, in the distance appeared another avenue of limes, leading to the river.

Belton in winter was hospitable and warm, with big log fires burning in the grates of polished steel and brass, silver candlesticks shining against the dark walls, and lamps illuminating the rooms.

Adelaide Lady Brownlow was a picturesque and beautiful figure. Her profile and her large grey eyes bespoke a generous but austere nature. The hair growing well off her high square forehead gave her a Jovian aspect. Her voice was husky and sweet, her carriage remarkably stately, her dress Italianate and magnificent. Lord Brownlow too was a handsome, soldierly figure, tall and bearded, with a stag-like air. His clever nervous hands reminded one that he was an artist. His laugh was catching and agreeable.

As delightful but more intimidating were visits to the Pembrokes at Wilton. True, Lady Pembroke was her cousin and in a way familiar, but the company was sure to be smart and well-dressed and there were problems at home to do with Papa and the village, and in the great world it seemed all so different. I do not think Adela knew then, or perhaps ever, that nearly everyone has problems, if not about 'Papa' then about something else. She travelled by train down the Wylye valley, with its encircling downs and its thatched villages and church towers, and would finally see the spire of Salisbury Cathedral set in its close and water meadows, with the town of Salisbury to the north. Then the little town of Wilton, the great park wall, and Wilton House itself, that fine stone house of many periods. She would alight from the carriage that met her at the station and find herself in the immense rooms and famous cubes and passages of Wilton, lit, in November, by shaded lamps; Cousin Gertrude could be warmly welcoming and amusing. She had more devilment than her brothers and sisters and an unmistakable laugh, rather hoarse but pleasant. Her portrait was painted about this time by Edward Clifford and it gives a little of her 'elf locks', fair and thick, her enigmatic eyes and smile, and rather large mouth. Lord Pembroke was younger than she, and handsome and very tall, a serious character and much beloved.

In 1881 Adela's diary describes a visit to the Worcester Festival,[1] but in such meagre terms that I must add my own recollections of a later date. The great music remains the same, if the company and the fashions have changed, and I have tried to put myself in her shoes and fancy the festival in the 'eighties.

> And the Gentiles shall come to Thy Light
> And Kings to the brightness of Thy Rising

Handel's music, with its clear, ordered framework, its pomps and crescendos, its definite changes from grandeur to sadness, are a vastness on which one can rest; it is like a ladder set up on earth, reaching by orderly steps to Heaven. It goes drumming through the Cathedral, with shouts and praises, assorting well with the Palladian tombs, with the urns and scrolls and the soaring Gothic arches. I know my mother felt pleasure in the building up of sounds and in contrapuntal movement. How often in later life, helped by my father to express herself, did she play and enjoy that music, and remembered Worcester and Gloucester Festivals. 'And bring glad tidings', and the long 'Amen' would lift itself with liquid notes. The rhythmic pulsations of Handel and Beethoven beat through the mind as one went out into the sunshine and September air outside the Cathedral, the assembled crowd of listeners becoming part of the music, while the rhythm quickened, got fuller and finally ceased. Now the crowd moving forward became just an assembly of well-to-do people dispersing, top hats were being put on, ladies in rustling dresses following one another out, little groups forming outside, while the sunshine fell on the smooth grass and on the stonework of the Cathedral. Horses were heard champing, bits jingling, and the coachmen muttered

[1] The Three Choirs Festival is held at Worcester, Gloucester and Hereford in turn.

'Hol' up' and 'Now then' to their horses, reminding one that carriages were being called, and the owners getting into them and driving away. Others walked off for a meal (cold pies, tarts, and jellies on great white tablecloths) in a neighbouring house in the Close.

At the end of the day's music, the Brockhampton party, with my mother Adela among them, would drive out of the Close, through the narrow streets of old brick houses, and back over the river, where from the bridge the Cathedral tower looks diminished; and upon the water below a few boats are seen and many swans, with their rippling reflections. Back along winding roads in the September evening they would go, light fleecy clouds in the sky and apples reddening in the green orchards. They would pass wooded slopes, misty in the distance and, nearby, grassy orchards with pear and apple trees covered with fruit, white geese and chickens upon the ground, and herds of red Herefordshire cattle with white faces. They passed signposts showing their open-sounding names, Martley and Whitbourne, Bromyard and Broadwas as they rolled along in the carriage; black and white houses with old brick chimney stacks appear, hopyards and oast-houses on the brackeny common, little squatters' cottages with pollard ash and damson trees overhanging clipped hedges and yews, often taller than the cottages. The road wound on, on one side a deep stream in its meadows. Turning into the Park the carriage would pass by the porticoed lodge (where in former years the family waited for the Worcester coach), and up the Brockhampton Drive to the house itself, standing sedate and trim.

One bundle of letters brings a whiff of the stableyard and the horsey world of Surtees and Alken, Jorrocks and *Mr Sponge's Sporting Tour*. Sometime after my grandmother's death, when he was getting old, grandpapa backed a bill for a horse dealer named Baker, who later went bankrupt and whose creditors called in the debt. My grandfather, belonging to an 18th-century framework, was easy-going, lordly and sporting; coaching days, with their smell of steaming horses and harness, will have come back to him as he stood about in Cheltenham stables or at Cheltenham sales and felt the horses' legs. Horses were his weakness and the dealers knew it very well. So, while Adela was reading books about social betterment, superintending a clothing club in the interest of Thrift, setting up a coffee house in the interest of Sobriety, and carefully keeping accounts, grandpapa (known in horsey circles as 'A nice gen'leman') was hobnobbing with the horse dealers at the *Plough*

Inn. Some of the letters dated 1880 describe how much perturbed were the family by papa's money transactions. Adela, for one, found herself in a frenzy of apprehension and fear of how things would look and how things would turn out. She consulted her brother George, since Gussy was in Ceylon. She consulted the discreeter cousins. Relations came to the rescue; the family circle stood firm. The Honourable and Reverend did not go bankrupt after all, but Adela had been through an experience she was never to forget.

She often felt at a loss, and had in mind to join a sisterhood and retire from the world. But this was never carried out, for the end of her lonely life at Withington was in sight. In 1885, staying with the Brownlows at Applecross in Scotland, she met her future husband, Charlton Lane, a handsome man of 49, parson, artist and athlete. His parish was close to Ashridge, the Brownlow's great house in Hertfordshire. The fact that he was liked by the Brownlow's circle no doubt gave him prestige in Adela's eyes as scholar and a sociable person, with great power of enjoyment, who gave as much as he took, and was amused at, and sympathetic to what he saw around him.

Although interested in other men she had met, and admired by them, Adela had never before unbent. Charlton Lane pressed his suit with devotion and gave her admiration and love, and she on her part, following the wishes of Lord and Lady Brownlow, began to rely on him for advice. She came to look up to him and to love him. His constant letters gave romance to her life at Withington, his buoyant nature sustained her and he taught her many things, chief of which was perhaps, that most of the tragedies of life come from stupidity.

Charlton Lane and his circle brought out in Adela a love of nature and of beauty which had lain dormant since Emma's death. The diary describing the visit to Applecross is full of descriptions of Scottish lochs and waterfalls, grey skies and mountains.

> We were enchanted with the wild beauty of the cliffs and rocks: I found 10 or 12 sorts of ferns among the rocks ... I made a sketch under Mr Lane's tuition ... the distant hills showed the most lovely lights and colouring.

The tall beautiful Adela came to life, she who had kept at arm's length other admirers, had thought of retiring from the world, and hitherto had made the arduous task of keeping Withington going her principal care.

Four

THE LANES OF ST MARK'S, KENNINGTON

My father's father, the Rev. Charlton Lane, had been the rector of St Mark's, Kennington, for 33 years in the early part of the 19th century. He was a scholarly urbane man, one of a family long connected with the city and hailing originally from Hitchendon in Buckinghamshire. At that time, fields and market gardens were to be found in the purlieus of Kennington, although the village itself had long since been swallowed up in the spread of London, and Vauxhall Gardens still existed as a place of entertainment. The long brown-coloured brick thoroughfare of Kennington High Street, built in the Regency period, looked much as it does today, except that the wagons of vegetables and fruit trundled along the cobbled street and over Vauxhall Bridge on the way to Covent Garden from the gardens of Surrey.

In the Rectory the Rev. Charlton Lane collected a library, adding to the books he had inherited from his father, from a Pollock grandfather, and from an uncle called Skottowe. His large and roomy church was late Regency in style, classical but with a flavour of Assyrian. A print, possibly of the day it was opened, shows the church with three-decker pulpit draped in red, horse-box pews and a congregation of ladies in bonnets and capes and men in drab frock coats, probably more elegant than the real congregation of small tradesmen and their families.

Mrs Lane was one of a family of seven sisters called Hill, of Wollaston Hall, Northamptonshire. In their youth they had travelled in Italy with their parents, and in Rome they were known as the 'Seven Hills of Rome'. Hers was a contented nature, and she made a happy home for her children, who were full of eager pursuits and interest in people, and had a predilection for music. The household was orderly, the Rector meticulous and careful, but with the easy ways of a settled thinker and the urbanity of a Christian. The five Lane children were Louisa, Charlton, Charles, Mary and William, a cheerful, well brought up crew.

The Rev. Charlton Lane.

The youngest, my uncle William, described the house to me when he
was 90 years old:

> The Parsonage itself was a dull as ditch-water, but there was a very
> nice garden, full of apples and pears, and a falling-to-pieces sort of
> stables. No, people like us didn't keep a carriage; when we wanted to
> get anywhere we went by bus. Every now and then someone came

Mrs Charlton Lane.

to see us in a carriage, and then it was put up in the stables. As to
the house, there was the dining room, the library ('it was a very nice
house' he put in irrelevantly, warming up) and the drawing room
opened on to the garden, and we children used to jump out from
the window. It was very nice for us to look on to the Oval from our
nursery windows and, yes, to see the balloons go up from Vauxhall
Gardens.

Perhaps it was thanks to this nursery view over the Oval that Uncle William later played cricket for Cambridge, and my father for Oxford.

> Looking across the Oval [went on Uncle Willy], I remember the balloon top rising over the houses. Mr Green was the balloon man's name. In those days there were no pavilion or buildings in the Oval, and the professionals used to bowl to us boys. When I was 12 I went to Westminster, and I used to run all the way to 8 o'clock school over Vauxhall Bridge. My mother used to give me a cup of tea before I started.

When I asked what my grandmother was like, Uncle Willy said, 'She was a dear, just like your father, everybody loved her.' I know she had light hazel eyes and a twinkling expression.

Later the Rev. Charlton Lane was given the living of the Parish Church, Hampstead, where he undoubtedly had a more cultivated congregation than at Kennington. He was a good Greek and Hebrew scholar, who went to original sources, not letting his thinking depend on the researches of others. He was well aware of the difference between the two 'ministries', of parish work and scholarship, as his letters to my father show. He wrote affectionate, self-revealing letters to his son, which have an 18th-century flavour, and show a scholarly mind, old-fashioned, but without absurdity.

Old volumes of Handel's music, of Italian opera, Rossini and Pergolese, reminded one of the musical pursuits of the Lanes; and a book of poetical pieces copied out by my grandmother as Miss Hill in Rome shows the usual polite enthusiasm for Byron.

My father was born in the London of Dickens, with its brown houses of brick, its smoky port of London, its Inns of Court, its City Companies, dark, narrow alleys and famous churches, its inns and its music halls – in Dickens' pages at least a jovial, pathetic scene with its own crooked beauty. To the boy of that day Dickens' works were as well known as Kipling's to the boy of today. London and the river were dirtier then than now, though doubtless more picturesque. The London fogs fell like a yellow pall in autumn and winter. Large as was the city, it was far easier then to get out into the country than it is today.

The Lane family belonged to the Mercers' Company, and Mercers' Hall has always played an important part in their lives and its chapel bore many of their names. The family has had its share in the civic life of London for centuries. One of the Lanes was Lord Mayor in 1697.

Charlton, my father, child of a happy home, combined the common-sense of the Lanes with the sensibility of the artist. He was sent to his first school at Ryde in the Isle of Wight, where he was very happy. At 10 he had begun his career as a cricketer. The yachts took his fancy at once, as his earliest letters show. He began to draw boats and later on at Oxford was to be not only a painter but an oar.

At about 13 my father returned to live at Kennington Parsonage, going to Westminster School as a day boy. The cloisters of Westminster show its monastic origin, as do the precincts of Westminster School. The Houses of Parliament, the river, the roaring streets, were all close by, but the wide-arched cloisters with green grass in the middle and the Abbey towering up on one side were quiet, echoing to the footsteps of the clerics, beadles and scholars, or to the leisured tread of sightseers. Here walked the Westminster boys; the Abbey was their Chapel, and its morning services their school prayers. It is one of the oldest schools in England, and certainly one of the most historic. My father played in the Westminster XI for five years, and was Captain in 1853. Dr Liddell was headmaster at that time.

When in 1856 my father went from London with its smoky skies, from Westminster School to Christ Church, Oxford, he entered a larger scholastic world. At Christ Church was the great quad with the Cathedral in one corner, the wide staircase, with its fan-tracery, leading up to the great Hall; and there was Christ Church Meadow, with its rich grass in summer, its sedgy streamlets, the winding tributary of the Thames flowing along one border and the Thames itself along another. There too were the great elms of the Main Walk, as much part of Oxford as the buildings themselves, and the willows, silver-leaved, flickering and lightening in sun and wind, and the poplars by Magdalen Tower. Oxford's skies, bred of river mists hanging over the city, have the brightness and variety of Pre-Raphaelite paintings, its sunsets the delicacy of Ruskin's watercolours. All these Charlton noted and enjoyed. He would have known the grey lanes running behind the main streets, Bear Lane, Cat Lane, The Turl, Longwall Street, and the High, with its grand curve which soon led into country roads. At times he would walk, painting satchel on back, to where, like the Scholar-Gypsy, he could look down on Oxford and trace its outline:

> Runs it not here, the track by Childsworth Farm,
> Past the high wood, to where the elm-tree crowns

> The hill behind whose ridge the sunset flames?
> The signal-elm, that looks on Ilsley Downs,
> The Vale, the three lone weirs, the youthful Thames?
> This winter-eve is warm,
> Humid the air! leafless, yet soft as spring,
> The tender purple spray on copse and briars!
> And that sweet city with her dreaming spires,
> She needs not June for beauty's heightening!

At other times, one of a crowd of black-gowned young men, my father hurried to lectures, past the inn-yards, the iron gateways, the church doors, to the echoing clang of church bells and clocks striking the hour, down the wagon-filled Cornmarket or the High, a-clatter with carriages, drays and coaches.

At Oxford Charlton made his beginning with watercolour – at Iffley, or in the Christ Church Meadow, or by the Thames, painting trees mirrored darkly in the water, barges lying low in the tide; or drawing the famous spires, towers and cupolas of Oxford itself, thrown up perhaps by a stormy sky when spring made its fluff of tiny leaves on the trees; or when, on October evenings, a rosy flush overspread the scene. Enjoyment led him to brood on what he saw and to put it on paper: sunshine falling on close foliage, throwing shadows, sharpening up angles of old cottages, of church towers and barns; or the shapes of distant sheep, men, cattle, hayricks, and birds in flight. Tiny clouds would drift above him, light airy winds blow among his papers, and birds' songs and lowing of beasts make an undertone to his work and to his thoughts. The poets empty of thought, the philosophers empty of sensation, ritual hymns of the church rolling in between, each had a turn in his mind. Later he fell in with the Pre-Raphaelites, and made friends with John Everett Millais, while Ruskin had a strong influence upon him and his painting. In the portfolios I find a sketch called 'A sprig of elder in autumn', a true Pre-Raphaelite study dated 'Oxford 1857'. Another with the same influence is 'The river at Newnham', then there is 'The wooden bridge at Putney', commemorating the boat race in which he rowed for two years, and 'My Home, Kennington Parsonage', a real Victorian record. In spring Magdalen Meadow showed fritillaries growing sparsely in the short grass, the purple-speckled heads of the flowers hanging bell-like on delicate curved stems, crested with sabre-like leaf, fluttering in spring winds; while others, white, shy and ghostlike, clustered in occasional groups, ready to open more fully under the glancing sun. March that brought the spring flowers to the painter, for the rowing men brought training in Christ Church Meadow in 'clear frosty morning air'.

My father was a fine athlete as well as an artist and with his handsome face and athletic figure had a quality that was almost Greek. He rowed in the University VIII and played in the University XI, being the first old Westminster Double Blue and one of the few Oxford Double Blues for rowing and cricket.

This athletic fame gave my father the detachment of success and the excitement of new friends, men whom he liked and who liked him. He appreciated his fellows, feeling that amusement, which is neither cynicism nor raillery, at their foibles, their love of ease, their pedantry and sensuality, while enjoying their virtues to the full. Among the records of this time, photographs of young men in stocks and chokers, holding tasselled caps or top hats, show him and his friends posing before the camera, then a new invention, with all the self-consciousness of youth.

Not his athletic prowess only, but his receptive mind made him popular at Christ Church. He was 'up' with the Prince of Wales and with the Lord Brownlow of the day. Each of these offered him a living, later, on his taking of orders. He chose that of his friend, Lord Brownlow.

To judge from the photographs, he found life none too easy at that time, in spite of his success in varying fields. The expression of the well-proportioned features shows the doubt and self-questionings of youth, indications of conflict, perhaps, between the athlete, the artist, and the son of loving parents at Kennington Parsonage. He certainly worked industriously at drawing and watercolour, and his sketches show a firm, delicate hand, and good craftsmanship; but he was not to be a painter by profession, for after some hesitation he was persuaded by his father to take orders. Did he find satisfaction in his chosen profession, one wonders? His name of 'Admirable Crichton' and the reputation he left behind him of a good fellow and staunch friend seem to show that he did.

The diary which he kept the second year he rowed in the Oxford crew against Cambridge, called 'The Log of 1859', may still be of interest to rowing men. In places he seems to be breathlessly rowing the course over again as he writes:

> After last year, which none of us old 'uns looked upon as defeat, we determined, in the words of our skipper 'to do our dirtiest' to lick Cambridge. The first thing this term was to select a crew from the two

Charlton Lane at Oxford.

trial crews of last term. The great Bellam, by running with us, was at last decided as to the 8 men, and we began immediately to go down regularly in the Ch-ch gig 8 whenever our torpid could spare her, and on the occasions when she was being used by our torpid, some other old screw was put to do the work. Our stroke was for some time a matter of doubt. John Arkell and Lawless, being the disputed men, I voted for old John because of his power of lasting and always doing his work conscientiously, whereas Lawless is naturally stiff in the back, which impedes the catching sharp at the beginning, and too young for the work. Till today, 23 March, we have been sometimes going between Iffley and Oxford, sometimes below Lock. Which is the least agreeable of the two I have not yet decided ... One's back a hundred yards thro' the railway bridge 40 a minute with the spurt for the last few hundred yards still in prospect. In that spurt, the first three strokes, one feels that one can preserve life to the end, but suddenly the backbone positively refuses to remain upright, but by a few more blobs in and out of the water the lasher is reached at last. At first going below locks was attended with considerable inconvenience owing to the wind which was awfully against us. But lately the weather has been such as to bring down our weights rapidly ... We did the course and 22, seven and a quarter. The rowing throughout was a great improvement, although we were pumped at the end. Such a lovely day for a walk, the sun shining and a cold wind blowing.

Tuesday. This afternoon we rowed over the long course with a very quick stroke, 39 to 40, time 22, 45. The weather at starting was lovely, but just as we got to Sandford Lock a tremendous storm was coming on. It predicted a ducking, half way to Nuneham. But till we got out of the boat at the Poplars not a drop of rain fell. Just then a violent hailstorm came on which lasted for a very short time. The atmospheric effects were very fine during this. I observed the lower clouds on the horizon were yellow. Over these lighter clouds the dark storm passed rapidly purple and brownish tint [and here the young artist-oar makes a rough sketch in the diary]. It was a case of pump today after the last spurt in going home. The clouds were glorious, a steely grey underneath away from the light, yellowish-pink towards the light, in fine rolling masses. Dinner very nicely done in Pembroke. Skipper dined with us. Wednesday, breakfast with John. Today we did not go down the long course as the crew were generally weak, but twice spurting to Iffley and back, with a run round the meadow, made a fair day's work for us. Robarts gave dinner.

Friday. A lovely morning round the meadow, no wind and a clear frosty morning air. At 11 the wind begins to rise and at 2 it blows like the devil. We rowed to Sandford and Pinckney steered us. The wind going out to Sandford Lock was so infernal that we had great difficulty in getting the boat out at all, and all over the course the wind unceasingly dead against us, except for a minute or two round Nuneham Island when the rudder was hard on. Time was bad in consequence, but I was happy in not being pumped. Dinner and breakfast this day with Baxter.

Saturday. The wind was not quite so bad as yesterday but the waves below the island at Nuneham made the rowing bad. Time 24, 7.

Sunday. New moon this morning, which I trust will bring less wind and more warmth for we want to come down a bit. Cambridge boasts of her seven old men. I hope we shall thrash them.

Monday. Wind against us as usual, time bad, the wind was blowing dead against us all the way down and the waves were tremendous.

Tuesday. Breakfast and dinner with Risley. Wind against us again, time 23, 45. Filthy row for the active concerned. Randle said we were in good time at the railway bridge.

Wednesday. Last day over the course. Wind against us as usual, a burning sun, I never was hotter in my life. We rowed down to Gut and back. A Cambridge man turned up, praised our opponents immensely. Robarts, John and I walked to Sandford to luncheon. We rowed over the course, time 23. Dined with Lonsdale.

Thursday. The Skipper, Robarts, Tommy and Risely in one carriage, John and I with two old gentlemen in the other compartment of the same carriage. A good deal of bear-fighting during the journer. We got to Putney at 12.30. A fearfully hot day, rowed over the course at 4.30. We were rather late for the tide at its strongest time, but the time was good, 21, 44. The bugs found me out during the night.

Friday. The weather has changed, being cooler and more wind. I spent the day reading and painting. We rowed at 6, wind against us and water very rough at Hammersmith. The time 22, 50. The Skipper dines with us tonight, which makes our evenings always jollier. Tommidge and I bought sundry copies of the Newgate Calendar and a china baby for John Arkell which was served up in a dish at dinner by itself. Baxter, Clarke and Morrison are such blokes not to talk and as old John is not very voluble in his conversation the addition of the Skipper's company is very jolly. We had great fun with old Captain [his dog] pushing him backwards and forwards on the slippery table. We finished the evening with a general bear-fight between the Skipper and Bob with a bandbox. Just as I was going to sleep I felt one of my old friends at me, so lighting a lucifer I transferred my carcass to the floor, placing the bed clothes over me, and so passed the night. I can't say I slept.

Saturday. Weather fearfully bad. Cambridge men came in the afternoon; we went out for a paddle in the morning about 11 o'clock and rowed at 6. The tide was not good. As we got thro' Hammersmith the waves were so high that we thought we must back, but on the whole the rowing was very good, especially after we had passed Barnes where the high banks sheltered us from the south-west wind. We ran back over the Common house. I arrived first by a good deal, Risley and John next. T. Egan said he liked the rowing very much.

Monday. The Cambridge men rowed over the course this morning for the first time. They were not so good in their paddle as in their spurt. Their time was 22, 40. Jack Hall rows as well as ever. The rest I did not think so much of. We tried the new oars this morning which did not suit some of us, but they are stiff and only want a slight alteration. Our time was 22, 59 from Ship to Searle. Risley and I went to London in the afternoon, I to Suffolk Street [a picture gallery], where I saw a great deal of very bad work. Vicat Cole is the only man who shows good work. In the evening we spurted to Hammersmith and had starts coming home.

Tuesday. A most splendid morning, sunshine and jolly breezes. I slept well for the first time since I have been in Putney, Bob and I changed beds. Cambridge went better this morning, their time was 22 min. We rowed as yesterday, directly after the Cantabs, up to Mortlake, turned round and spurted back directly we met them coming thro' Barnes Bridge. The oars were better today and the rowing too. John does not row an easy stroke, especially for the paddle, and in a spurt it is not enough marked. Bow side were before stroke today nearly all the way. The time from Ship to Searle's 20,50, but we, when rowing from Mortlake to Putney, always start from Barker's rails. Finished Bellam's picture this morning. Did portrait of Captain O'Marn [the dog] and went with Tummidge to Kew Gardens. It rained and blew so it was not very agreeable.

Wednesday. Our last row over the course, a deal of wind. Cambridge rowed the Waterman's course this morning. We started first, and went thro' the waves to Mortlake in a promising manner, in fact I was quite surprised to find myself at the end of the course.

Thursday. Lovely morning. We practised starts. Went to be photographed. Lunched with Skipper, British Institution. Betting 5 to 3 on Cambridge. It is regarded as a certainty.

Friday 15th. The eventful day. Windy this morning when I ran. Cantabs were not over pleased with the weather evidently, however it is what we prayed for. Freeman, Baring, Thesiger and others came up to see us. I passed the morning packing, but such was one's excitement that I could not remember what to pack up and what to leave. 12 and a quarter, 'We must go to the boat house. Come on!' Down we trot with confidence, but looked at as doomed creatures, pity and scorn depicted on everybody's face. We put our boat in the water and row thro' the frightful swell to the Aqueduct. The Cantabs have not got their boat in yet. There is no movement in the crowd round Searle's yard betokening the coming of the enemy. It's getting very cold, snow falling. At 1 o'clock the Light Blue comes to the post. They row thro' the bridge and after 10 minutes the other side of the bridge they prepare for the start. 'Do you fellows want to be swamped?' says Judas Williams. 'Can't you swim?' say I. 'Are you ready?' 'No! No! No!' say Cantabs. Now we're off! 'Hold your oars tight! Well forward. Feather high!' Now we are ahead. Can it be possible? Our condition must be better, so if we are once ahead, well we can keep it. Here we go! A boat's length at Hammersmith! 'Well rowed 3' shouts a voice on the bank. It's Fred Marshall. At Coney Hatch Cantabs put on a deathlike struggle. Keep it long!!! Keep it long! 'Go home old man, go home!!!' say we all under Barnes Bridge ...

Oxford won the race.

Five

TRAVELS AND TWO CURACIES

The next year, the year he came down, father was captain of the Oxford XI, and the same summer he went to Ireland to play cricket for the Zingari. His diary at the time shows his 'joie de vivre' and his feeling for the landscape.

> The view from Conway was lovely [he writes of the journey]. The river of the deepest blue reflecting the sky, and the distant clouds had formed themselves into piling masses folding around the tops of the farthest hills. The mountains a lovely pale purple, leading the eye into the heart of Snowdonia, the foreground composed of a green back of trees, already in some places showing that autumn had begun. On the other hand the Orme's Head stood out boldly and showed his rough sides in the loveliest light and shade. On arriving at Holyhead a calm passage seemed in prospect.

The team was to stay at Viceregal Lodge with Lord Carlisle, the Viceroy.

> We got late to Dublin, but Fred Marshall had kindly sent his servant to meet me and he brought me to the Lodge. Supper had been prepared for me, we smoked a cigar in the aide-de-camp's room and then retired to bed.
>
> Monday. A match with the Guards (1st Battalion). I stayed indoors and finished some drawings. His Ex. was kind enough to pay me a visit and said, 'You know how much pleasure it gives me to have you here.'

My father's first job, on leaving Oxford, appears to have been tutoring his friend Lord Brownlow's younger brother, Adelbert Cust. The Christmas following the visit to Dublin found my father at Castle Ashby, Northamptonshire, which belonged to Cust's uncle, Lord Northampton.

Here my father began his life-long friendship with Lady Marion Alford (Lady Marion Compton m.1841 John Viscount Alford, eldest son of John, 1st Earl Brownlow), his pupil's mother, and here too he met her brother, Lord Alwyne Compton, who was a clergyman, and his wife, a daughter of Bishop Alexander. In his diary I find: 'We spent Xmas this year at Castle Ashby, and very comfortable we were. Lord Northampton was very agreeable, draws beautifully. Great fun decorating the church on Xmas Eve with Lady Alwyne.' We spend the evenings in copying coats of arms for Lady Alwyne. From Castle Ashby, my father seems to have visited Ashridge, Lady Marion's home in Hertfordshire, for the first time. After the above comes, 'Paid a visit to Raglan Somerset while at Ashridge. He sent me *Steps to Heaven* by Keble, so kind of him!'

Early in the following year my father and his pupil, and Lord Alwyne Compton, joined Lady Marion Alford and Lady Alwyne in Rome. The diary goes on:

Jan 24, 1861. Lord Alwyn, Addy [Hon. Adelbert Cust] and I started last Friday evening from London, having for a courier one Gustave. A calm passage from Folkestone to Calais, and an early journey from Calais to Paris. Reached Paris at 8 a.m. on Saturday – *Hotel Bristol.* After washing, we proceeded to the Louvre – a good picture of Decamps there – sunrise effects against low-lying or rising ground, river underneath. I can now admire Veronese, and Raphael and Titian ('Deposition') more than formerly. Francia's head of a man, and Leonardo's woman to be remembered for ever. Dined at Philip's restaurant, good dinner, Mr Gurney's church in the morning.

Sunday. High Churchman, nice service – walked Bois de Boulogne in afternoon. Left Paris on Sunday, bad night in the train, although we got the coupé to ourselves. Awake all night. Thought of many dodges for supporting my head with straps – unsuccessful however.

Monday. Fine but windy. Breakfast at Lyons at 7.30, lunch at Avignon – capital table d'hote. In the afternoon we passed through some very fine scenery along the Rhone which we sketched going along. Marseilles at 3.30, *Hotel des Colonies.* The streets are very picturesque, especially at sunset when the rich lights and dark shadows make much showy contrasts. Left Marseilles at 10 o'clock after a good dinner at hotel, during the whole of which we were regaled by a woman singing to her child some pretty country songs. After dinner we went to a Café Chantant, taken there by Gustave. Walked to steamer with difficulty owing to the high wind which nearly blew us off our legs!

The first view in the morning from the deck quite enchanting – sea indigo with high waves, green, glimmering towards the summit, and in the distance the mountains of Carrara, snow-capped. The wind increased during every hour, rendering our condition doubtful. The wretched soldiers (French, 350) all lying about on deck – their dinner very curious, eating and 'catting' and drinking and smoking. At 5.30 dinner announced – we went below. I immediately left the saloon. Ate a roll on deck, stayed an hour above and then to roost. I brought up my roll and then slept. I found Addy and Lord A. already lying down. In the morning we expected to arrive in time to get off from Civita Vecchia but the sea had strained the engines in the night, and obliged us to put into Elba, which delayed our arrival. I was asleep at the time and did not see Elba except in the distance [he writes to his sister], the Courier pointed it out to me the next day. I could see only a faint blue line of mountains against the sky. The sea was the most enchanting colour. The trough of the waves dark indigo and the foam of the breaking waves made streaks of bright emerald green on it.

The peculiar smell of an Italian town first felt at Civita Vecchia, pleasant from association. Rome at 4.30, lovely sunset, a feeling of being really in the Eternal City, quite curious, how delightful.

Wednesday. In morning walked about to find horses. In afternoon we drove to baths of Caracella, such a view! Such a sunset! Came home and began a drawing of the sunset from our window. Went to a capital concert at 7 o'clock. Mlle. Parrisotti, beautiful contralto voice. She sang 'Lascia ch'io pianga', Handel; and 'Il mio sospiro', Donizetti. King of Naples expected to come to Rome today.

Lady Marion and the Alwyne Comptons, already figures in Roman society, were well versed in the English-Roman tradition; while young Cust, newly emancipated from Eton and destined for the Guards, was learning about the Italian schools of painting and drawing himself, though his mother's passion for galleries sometimes induced a weariness of spirit. In the intervals of tutoring young Cust, my father turned over in his mind what his own profession should be. Now he would join the Guards, now he would be a painter, but the Church was the strongest attraction, and would afford some leisure for his painting. Humorous and sensible, no longer a 'tame cat' as at Castle Ashby, he joined in all the enthusiasms of his hosts, writing his diary and filling some sketch books with drawings and caricatures. Rome, once familiar to his mother (one of the 'seven Hills of Rome') filled his mind, prepared as he was by the classical education of Westminster and Oxford.

He worked at a studio in Rome. The diary tells that:

> Lady Marion proposed in the morning [two days after their arrival], that we should all go to a drawing class, so we called on Marianecci but he was not at home, from thence to Gibson's studio to see 'Pandora' which is exceedingly beautiful. At first I did not sympathize with the extravagant praise given to it, but after careful observation I saw that it had expression of face and that the tout-ensemble showed great taste, and the drapery well rendered.
>
> Miss Hosmer's studio afterwards. Her 'Captive Queen' is fine and her 'Puck' which is the Prince's [of Wales]. In the afternoon we visited St Peter's. The style is certainly not so adapted for church architecture as Gothic, but the massive size and the richness of marbles makes the effect grand in the extreme – looking up into the Dome, what a height it seems! It is scarcely credible that all those pictures are mosaics – they are so rich in colour and the drawing is just like oil painting. Some of the monuments of the Popes are very fine.
>
> The outside I do not admire so much, the columns appear crowded with windows. It was altered from Michael Angelo's original plan ...
>
> Tuesday. To the Medici Gardens in the morning to finish a sketch – how fine the ilexes are here! In packing up my drawing materials to start home again I dropped my case of brushes and was obliged to walk all round by the Piazzo del Popola to pick it up. In the afternoon we went to the Pamphile Doria – the weather was showery and the large grey clouds darkened the view towards evening, the clouds went away to the Alban Hills and a lovely sunset repaid us for waiting – all the prominent parts of the landscape were caught by the glowing light forming lively bright spots amid the grey gloom of the ilex woods and the twisted arms of the stone pines.

Now follows Roman Society again. In a letter to his sister Mary, my father writes:

> The galleries are mostly belonging to old Roman families. The pictures were collected by the patrons of the great Italian artists who lived in the 14th and 15th centuries, the Borghese, Doria, Farnese and Colonna families, who once were really great and patronised art to an immense extent, although they fought so much with each

other. You should see the representatives of these families now, quite equal to their ancestors in pride, but in appearance a great falling-off has taken place. They have very large houses in Rome but they live in a most uncomfortable way, quite at the top of them. They most of them have villas out of the city which they go to in the summer when Rome is unbearably hot. The villas are beautifully adorned with sculptures and old bas-reliefs in most cases bought by the Cardinals of the family who, being unshackled by family ties, spent their time and money on enriching their houses, thereby conferring an immense boon on their descendants. These sculptures are what were brought from Athens, Corinth and Agrigentum and other Greek towns by the ancient Romans, especially at the time of Augustus, to embellish their houses. But when the Goths destroyed Rome these sculptures were lost, some buried and some knocked to pieces. By degrees they were dug up. There are still beyond doubt countless treasures below the surface of the earth, but the Papal government won't allow any foreigners to dig or excavate at all. There is a pleasant society of artists here, Gibson and Macdonald being the great sculptors. Gibson is really a great artist. His Venus is one of the most beautiful statues I ever saw, only surpassed by the Venus of the Capitol. There is a curious little American female sculptor, a Miss Hosmer, who by her talents and independence of character has made a name here. She is a friend of Lady Marion's and is doing at present a bust of Lady Alwyne as a present for Lady Marion. She dresses very like a man, except trousers, wearing her hair short.

Miss Hosmer has already appeared in Emma Talbot's letters. The diary goes on:

In the evening we went to Miss Hosmer's. Browning was there. He is very agreeable, small, but well-made and clever-looking. The room in which she received us is her bedroom. It is prettily and tastefully fitted up, with several of Gibson's sketches and some magnificent casts.

Monday. Drawing lesson. To Lungezza with Lady M. and Addy. Very beautiful it is. The early greens of the willows so lovely. Such a classical atmosphere about the place. Reminded one of Virgil and Horace. Here one might fancy the shepherds in the golden age living their happy life. The long purple shadows creeping up the mountains, the dark green and purple streaks on the Campagna, the bright green of the willows by the watercourses, made such lovely pictures.

Wednesday. We walked in the afternoon about the Campagna. Browning's lines come to the mind:

> The champaign with its endless fleece
> Of feathery grasses everywhere!
> Silence and passion, joy and peace,
> An everlasting wash of air –
> Rome's ghost since her decease.
>
> Such life there, through such lengths of hours,
> Such miracles performed in play,
> Such primal naked forms of flowers,
> Such letting Nature have her way
> While Heaven looks from its towers!

Thursday. Drawing lesson. Rode to Cicero's villa. A reception night (at Lady Marion's). Browning was agreeable.

Friday. Mr Knight drove us in his drag to Tivoli. The sun shone but the wind was cold. The view of the town improves as you approach it. The olive woods, hoary in the wind, with their gnarled trunks are immensely picturesque. I longed to paint a study of them. We went to Villa d'Este.

He knows how to describe a classical landscape either in words or with pencil and brush.

How beautiful the view each way is! On one side the eye ranged over miles of olive wood and campagna to the Alban Hills, on the other, cypress, weeping-willow and several other kinds of trees, each with a different green, enriched the foreground, beyond which the pretty town stands up on the brow of the hill. We walked to the Cascatela down the prettiest of roads, upon which came groups of the brightest dressed women and heavily laden beasts casting long shadows on the uneven road. The evening effect was superb. Looking up from the bed of the Anio you saw the hills on the right glowing in light, crowned by the town. The thickly wooded hill on the left was in shadow, and shaded the opposite one.

Interesting company again:

Browning dined with us, also Miss Hosmer. Browning is a great talker, but talks well. He acts as a sort of guardian to Savage Landor, who is now 80 and lives at Florence. He is mad and his money is taken care of for him, for otherwise he would be throwing it away in all directions. Browning's knowledge of the classics is very great and he writes Latin verses with as much ease as he does English. He was speaking of Shelley, and of Trelawney's life of him as being so false throughout. Trelawney is a noted liar. He has travelled about a good deal and report says he has married four wives. The first two he disposed of by strangling, number one with her own hair, number two by eating her. He ran away with a man's daughter at Florence, the father pursued the guilty pair into the room where they were dining and began by demanding back his daughter. 'Before proceeding (says Trelawney) pray try this port wine, sir!' – 'Really this is abominable!' – 'Oh, do let me implore you to try this wine' – then glass number two, etc. etc.!

The artist notes many kinds of beauty, this time that of flowers.

Wednesday. Mr Knight drove us to Ostia. Very picturesque, especially the walk down to the sea which is scented with flowers. A heavy thunderstorm threatened us, but luckily it passed away from us, waterspouts, and all. Browning's story about the Orleanist arrangement is amusing. Their enemies say of them 'ils pechent toujours à la ligne!' The walk that we took from the house at Fazano down to the sea is very lovely, such thickness of trees and underneath cyclamen, daphne, myrtle, violets and rosemary grew in the wildest luxuriance. Numbers of wild-looking inhabitants of the sea shore attacked us for baiocci.

The antiquarian side of my father is delighted with missals and woodcuts.

Wednesday. In the afternoon Mr Gray took me to the Minerva Library. We were shown several interesting and beautifully illustrated missals, hymnaria etc. of about the 9th century and the liberal present of a queen's head to the under-librarian, which diverted and gratified him immensely, made him very attentive. A splendid collection of Albert Dürer's woodcuts please me greatly. I never saw him so grand before, the drawing and composition so wonderful. From the garden we saw the most exquisite effect of colour on the mountains, which I attempted. To the top of the church tower where a grand view of country under the gorgeous colours of a thundery evening delighted us.

Val Prinsep was one of the Pre-Raphaelite group, a handsome youth at this time.

I went with Prinsep to Albano. We started on the most glorious of mornings, the Campagna dewy, glistening and misty, the mountains clear, well-defined but pale. After breakfast at our hotel we journeyed along the right side of the valley of Lariccia, treading amidst beds of marigolds which grew under the young olives. We sketched Ariccia. It looked so Turneresque against the early sky, sun slanting on the brown roofs through the smoke. I was astounded at the beauty of Castel Grandolfo's position. Up early next morning, finished drawing of Arricia and began one of the road. After lunch to the lake. Toiled at the drawing of the bank. The tone is so difficult to get. It is not purple and not green and the drawing is distinct and yet subdued. Having finished, Val and I walked along that lovely avenue of ilexes, enlivened by the bright dresses and faces of children which lit up the gloom of the sombre foliage. Coming to the town as the sun was setting we commanded from the bridge a magnificent view of the Campagna. From the terrace on the right of the town we looked into the lake which reflected the moon while the sun yet burnt on the opposite mountain.

The drawings my father did, at once vigorous and delicate, influenced by Claude Lorrain and Ruskin, convey the impression of Italian landscape with its many individual scenes in one sweep: the vineyard, the convent garden, the forest, the ruin, the distant mountains. He had the Romantic Victorian's appetite for detail. These Roman studies carry one back to the Classical age.

During Passion Week there was a great deal to be seen and heard. I heard an hour's 'Lamentation' in St Peter's and left tired before the 'Miserere'. The Day of the Benediction was very interesting. Mixing with the crowd in St Peter's I saw several fine costumes, for the crowd was of a very motley character, numbers of peasants who were evidently new to the scene, priests and friars of every denomination, ladies and gentlemen, foreigners and English. The blue steel and silver ornamented armour of the Swiss Guard officers is handsome. I was rather disappointed with the silver trumpets. The singing of the chorus was beautiful resembling chimes. But there was no jarring of notes or unpleasant effect, the harmony swelled and died through the great dome. The Benediction was not successful as the rain came on and the crowd was not very large. The Piazza was chiefly filled with soldiers. The illumination of St Peter's is grand, and the fireworks are capital, especially the last effect of shooting comets over the heads of the crowd, which by the way was almost entirely composed of French soldiers.

Venice. Spent a pleasant evening with Rawden Browne, who read us curious letters collected by him from the library of St Mark. They were relative to Queen Elizabeth's anxiety to have an ambassador from Venice. Her petulance to the young Secretary of the Venetian Embassy is amusing. His discoveries about *Don Quixote* are curious, that it's a political satire. Cervantes was imprisoned for satirising the Duke of Lerma as Don Quixote. It is known the Duke had a fit of melancholy (Knight of the Rueful Countenance). Francezza, who had been born a slave on the Lerma estates, was Sancho Panza. Archbishop of Toledo was the Curate.

   We spent an agreeable evening at Danieli's with the Lothians. How delightful Lady Lothian is, and how cheerful and beautiful Lady Adelaide [Talbot: afterwards Lady Brownlow]. She must be great fun when her shyness works off. Poor Lothian takes immense interest in what he sees, but what a cripple.

This is the first allusion to the Talbot family in my father's papers.

   In 1862, a year after returning from Italy, my father was ordained, and took his first curacy at Great Whitley in Worcestershire. It is a country of rolling commons, hills and small farms – and 'little bits of sportive wood run wild'. The landscape is almost Italian in variety, many coloured – valleys, river beds, tufted hillocks, orchards, and hop-yards opening up as vistas to the eye, as one travels through it, now on this side and now on that.

   My father did many paintings of this countryside, still in the Pre-Raphaelite manner, carefully drawn and brightly coloured. There is warmth and light in the sketches, the distances recede and the nearby cottages and trees are put in with a sure and intimate touch, making delightful pictures.

   Still faithful to the aristocracy, Lane went with young Lord Ellesmere in 1865 – again to Italy, whence he writes to his mother:

Hotel Danieli, Venice, 2 May 1865

My dear Mother,
   In my last letter I said we proposed spending this Sunday at the City of Palaces, you see by my date we have accomplished our end. I wrote from Maggiori, I think. Our route from thence lay through Lugano. Leaving Pallanza, which is by far the best place to stop at on Maggiore, being situated just at the apex of the angle of land which runs into the middle of the lake and so commanding a fair view either down or up; we came down to Luino by steamer, from Luino by

carriage to Lugano, thence by steamer up the Lake to Portezza, thence by an hour's carriage to Menaggio. Then Cenis first appeared spread out in soft violet indistinctness backed by sharp angular mountains where tops and shoulders were smitten with evening glory and deep hollows filled with loveliest sapphire. While on the water we heard the many churches of the villages which dotted the shores and climbed the steep hillsides and the white-walled monasteries high up like white birds on the crags, giving out their deep voices calling to evening prayer. It is remarkable how fine the bells of Italy are in tone; few churches have more than two, many only one, but yet always, as far as I know, rich and fine in tone.

From Bellagio, where we spent two pleasant days, we journeyed to Verona. There is much to see there, the churches are good and specimens of Lombardic architecture, which is rude in execution compared with the Renaissance, but full of power indicative of the stern character of that Lombard people who first ruthlessly destroyed the Christian Church and monasteries from north to south of Italy but, after they were converted, chiefly by the instrumentality of the Benedictines, threw their strength and fierceness into the service of the Church. Verona to Venice yesterday. This beautiful city is by no means new to me, but I delight more in it now than before. A better knowledge of its history and its art makes one appreciate it more. An American asked me last night what my first impression of Venice was. 'Mine,' he said, 'is that it is exceedingly dirty.' Such people ought to stop at home. The dirt here adds to the charm of the place, it proclaims it history, for it comes from the brine of the sea, the stain of salt waves; these stains are eloquent of her once maritime power, now passed away, they teach all who visit her the deep lesson of the sure fall of pride and fullness and want of faith in the Giver of wealth and increase.

What shall it profit a nation if it gain the whole world and lose its own soul.

I constantly wish that you and my father were with me. What a treat it would be to both to see these beauties of nature and art. Goodbye.

With love to you all, Your aff. son

P.S. think of me specially next Sunday week which is St Barnabas Day [his birthday]

In the Easter of 1866 Lane went to France as tutor to young Leveson Gower, son of the Duke of Sutherland, and writes to his mother:

24 June 1866, Le Mans, France

My dear Mother,

I received your last letter at Avranches which entertained and amused me. I was much amused at the idea of the Princess Mary and Co. storming Nettleden Church. The church is so small and the congregation so completely rustic and savouring of the soil, that the picture presented by your letter of this grand dame and her magnificent German spouse, moustachioed and girt around with superb flunkies, marching down the church (probably rather late) is very rich – the yokels all aghast and astare. The Princess rather enjoying the fuss. I concluded that Princess Mary would choose to go to Nettleden as she knows Cautley [the Rector] to be so intimate at Ashridge.

(Princess Mary of Teck was a friend of Lady Marion Alford and, with her husband the Duke of Teck, often stayed at Ashridge.)

I have not said much about my companion, because it really takes a week or so to know him. He is like most English men, very shy naturally tho' so well mannered that it does not make him awkward, but makes him rather reticent and reserved. He has an amiable disposition, is evidently very fond of his mother to whom he frequently writes. His bringing up has been carefully attended to, for he is very right-minded and high-principled. This morning as there is no English service he and I read the morning service. He seemed to like the idea and to enter into it gladly. He shares with his family in a great admiration for Mr Gladstone personally and such a high-minded character as Gladstone must be so valuable in setting the tone of that society which so looks up to him. One is reminded of the vast responsibility of the position of such men, how their example has an unknown effect for good or otherwise. I am amused at the impression which pervades the Sutherland family that Gladstone is a great friend of mine. L. Gower said to me the other day, 'You know Mr Gladstone very well indeed.' He must have expressed himself kindly about me to the Duchess, for I didn't pretend to his friendship merely on the strength of our curious adventure last year.

This refers to a meeting about a ward of Mr Gladstone's.

I think it was kind of Gladstone, that when he was leaving the room at Chiswick he came back and asked the Duchess to be kindly remembered to me. The Duchess was afraid she had forgotten to tell me this, and sent word to her son to deliver the message. L. Gower and I have been reading Palgrave, as I think I mentioned to you, we like it very much, it is especially interesting here in this country. He is very good in describing the great conflict between the church and the throne which was fought between Rufus and Anselm. This you will read about in Hook. I doubt whether it is so graphically written as in Palgrave. This conflict which is so grievously misinterpreted in all the common histories that I know of, is particularly useful to study now when there is the same disposition to act as Rufus desired to act, tho' in a less ferocious spirit. The spirit of positive civilisation is now opposed to Christianity, and in all parts of Christendom it is anxious to make religion its slave. In England a desire exists to confiscate church property and to eliminate religious teaching from the State. Italy is hourly becoming irreligious; it is in some respects a good thing that the monasteries should be suppressed, but the spirit in which it is done is unsatisfactory. I am glad to hear that, at the suggestion of the Duchess of Sutherland, Garibaldi has promised to try and save Monte Cassino and Subiaco, which surely have not deserved to be confiscated.

After Havre we visited Falaise, a grandly situated castle, perched on a lofty rock; here William the Conqueror was born, and it became the Palace of the Norman Duchy, instead of the former one at Rouen. From the great round tower which Talbot built [another reference to the family he was later to marry into], 'you overlook a beautiful scene of rocky hills and deep rich valleys and distant towns and towering minsters; from Falaise we came to Caen, where William is buried in the magnificent cathedral built by Odo, Archbishop of Rouen, half-brother of William the Conqueror, and the famous Tapestries worked by the good Matilda, William's wife, and her ladies, descriptive of the events of the Conquest. It is most curious; there, in capital preservation, stands out the course of events graphically written in canvas in beautiful colour, the figures very quaint and out of drawing, but very life-like and telling the story admirably. I had no idea that there was so much of it; it takes about half an hour to interpret it all carefully. From Bayeux we came to Coutances to see the cathedral, thence the same day to Granville and early next day to Avrances, where we lunched, to journey on in the afternoon to Mt St Michel. We were so lucky in our weather there. It is so interesting in history and grand in the picturesque situation.

The church which crowns the summit of the rock is a fine Norman structure, and the Refectory of the monks, the Hall of the Chavaliers instituted by Louis XI, are beautiful specimens of pure Gothic art. We slept there in the little inn at the foot of the rock. I rose at 3.30

yesterday morning and saw the sun rise above the hills of Normandy and strike his first splendour on the rock of Mt St Michel. It was a grand morning and I felt repaid for my early rising. Here we came last night. This is interesting as it was once the capital of the Duchy of Maine. Tomorrow we visit Angers in Anjou thence along the Loire to Paris. As I shall probably be at home this week Friday or Saturday, I shall not look for another letter from you, I am just writing to the Duchess of Sutherland, so goodbye, au revoir,

With best love, Your affect. son

C.G. Lane

In 1866 my father became curate of Little Gaddesden, on the borders of Buckinghamshire and Hertfordshire, near his friends the Brownlows at Ashridge. Here he lived in an old gabled house called Robin Hood which had been an inn, where his sister Mary kept house for him. The rector at Little Gaddesden then was an old character called Mr Jenks. The Ashridge estate fell roughly between the market towns of Hemel Hempstead, Berkhamsted and Tring.

The ancient town of Berkhamsted then had a long high street of low houses of all shapes, broken at one point by the church of flint and stone, and its churchyard yew trees, while behind it stood the Henry VII grammar school of red brick. Outside the town a circle of ruined ivy-covered walls marked where an important medieval fortress had once stood, guarding a gap in the Chiltern Hills. There great beeches stood along the old ramparts, and hung over the reedy moat where floated an occasional swan. Alders leant towards the road, and whitethroats, wagtails and chaffinches flew in and out among the branches. A steep road led to the high ground of Berkhamsted Common, covered with gorse, yellow and warm-smelling, and hawthorn bushes, unbelievably white and lovely in May. Here one could go many miles at a stretch on foot, or on horseback, from Potten End to Ashridge or Aldbury Hill. Here my father walked and rode and here he made sketches of shepherds with their sheep, of gorse, with oak and beech trees against the skyline. To gallop along one of the grass rides, bracken and distant beech trees flying past, and arrive at the top of Aldbury Hill, to draw rein and look over the Vale of Aylesbury stretched beneath, gives a fine feeling of space and air. In winter and spring the wind rushes past one, the branches of the trees toss and sway, and as often as not the smell of bracken and moss refreshes one's senses, or in autumn the magical smell of burning leaves.

There are spread out the old villages, whose inhabitants have for centuries cultivated the soil of the Vale, have cut the great trees, and tended sheep upon the slopes of the chalk downs. There are the church towers of Ivinghoe, Edlesborough, Ellesborough, Pitstone, Long Marston.

The estate was a fair specimen of the big properties into which much of England was divided. In Lady Marion Alford's day the building of schools and churches, rectories and almshouses, farms and cottages went forward apace. It is true many ancient houses were pulled down, an energetic clerk of the works seeing to that. He was Paxton, brother to the famous Joseph Paxton, who built the Crystal Palace on the model of the glass houses at Chatsworth. The new buildings were not of an inspiring character, being an adaptation of Ruskinian Gothic, but the desire to improve conditions and make life more orderly did achieve results; Little Gaddesden at any rate became a model village. Lady Marion spent a great deal of money upon her cottages and schools.

This same lady and her eldest son (John Lord Brownlow, my father's friend and patron) drew upon themselves the indignation of Berkhamsted by attempting to enclose part of Berkhamsted Common. Lady Marion's letter to my father in 1866 on the subject is not without interest:

> … Brownlow only wishes to know what are his rights and what are not. The clique of gentlemen who are against him have talked themselves crazy. I am anxious to know what Brownlow may or many not do on the Common. If it turns out he has no rights to the Common (which is *impossible*) I hope he will leave it as it is. Certainly he will do everything to beautify it. It is curious to see the change of the last three years – before the cry was 'Enclose – enclose, it is a sin to leave land uncultivated – none but wicked baronial feudal tyrants can wish to have good land uncultivated, that they must only hunt over it and breed game'. Custom, custom! Suddenly it is discovered the baronial tyrants wish to keep the commons beautiful – but not to have them cut up – so now the cry is 'Wicked Barons must not enclose! But be ousted out of their wicked rights if they have any, over commons'.
>
> This rose first round London, now a little town like Berkhamsted is so afraid of becoming a London in size that it must preserve commons for lungs. Not for the breathing of the people but that they may cry aloud 'This we have saved from the wicked Barons who would not enclose when we wished it.' They none of them remembered that Brownlow has saved the commons from a building company …

After two years at Little Gaddesden my father became curate of Edlesborough in Buckinghamshire, nearby, where he lived at the foot of the Downs at a farmhouse called Wardshurst. Edlesborough village is below the Ivinghoe Downs, and has a beautiful Early English church set on a green hillock, a landmark in the Vale of Aylesbury. Surrounded by farms, with the sheep run of the Downs and the fine woods and park of Ashridge nearby, it was a picturesque setting for the landscape-painting young parson who, Londoner as he was, had come to enjoy country life.

In February the landscape appeared as dun-coloured slopes shot with green, the flocks of sheep hardly showing in the fields till the sun came out, giving each woolly form its own shadow. Bushes and hedges, spiky and brown, are ready to bring forth buds, and on the commons light brown bracken, so lately broken down, and covered with snow, forms a bed from which young fern would presently spring. As the year drew on, there were gypsy encampments, and my father would make notes of them in his sketch book, in the dusk, the little fire burning on the grass by the roadside and the hooded cart standing by.

In the shallow valley the streams, deep blue where the sky above is clear, are fringed here with bright green watercress, there with pale bleached grass, the woods are a soft fringe on the skyline, their outline dipping with the folds of the ground. Perhaps a pair of horses is drawing the harrow over the fields, driven with reins of rope by a ploughman. A magpie hops like a toy among the grassy tussocks. Lower down by the stream are rough tasselly alders. Pale primroses nestle in the hedges that skirt the young green cornfields. In one of the fields is a light ochre strawrick whose yellow rings stand out against the shaded blue of the sky, with white clouds at the horizon – flowing up to a zenith of pure azure.

In those early days of the year the grey green of the chalk hills, the close crops, the sheep folds in the fields, with the feathery trees of the Vale and the full bosky trees of the woods, brought some delightful sketches from my father's hand.

In late spring the 'terra-verte' of the Downs is splashed with the white of hawthorn bushes and yellow powdering of cowslips – sheep and lambs wander hither and thither cropping and bleating, the rough yellow of the gorse breaks the smooth hillside – young beeches in the Coombe Wood are fairy-like, so delicate is the yellow green of their silken leaves as they unfold.

From Edlesborough my father seems often to have ridden up Studham Hill to visit Lord and Lady William Compton and their daughters at Studham, and in his now much shorter diaries he made the entries 'lunched at Studham' and 'Lady William and Miss Compton called' – he was undoubtedly charmed by Katie Compton. Later on is 'Miss Compton's wedding' (Oct. 1870) and this, her marriage to Lord Cowper of Pansanger, must have ended these particular fancies which, though fruitless in one direction, had none the less served to give romance to the flowing landscapes of the Ivinghoe Downs.

A further memento is a photograph of the two Miss Comptons, Katie and Margaret, in full white muslin dresses, with their young brother Willy, afterwards Lord Northampton, seated outside the library on the stone terrace that runs round the house at Ashridge. The sleek heads, the white folds of the dresses, the demure and serious looks of the young sisters, with the Gothic arches behind them, have a curious beauty and look of permanence.

Ashridge then, as for many years to come, was a welcoming home for relations and friends. Another boy to whom my father was tutor was Lord Archie Campbell, son of the Duke of Argyll. In October 1866 is the entry 'Campbell came', in February 'Lady Compton called with Miss Minnie'. In October:

> Plays at Ashridge, *Morning Call* – and *Bengal Tiger*, Miss Compton and Addy acted *Morning Call* – both very good. *Bengal Tiger* – Colonel Eliot – Brownlow – Addy, Miss Minnie, Macnamara – Miss Boyle. The conservatory looked very pretty filled with neighbours, all seemed happy.

The play was acted in the orangery, a wing of the great house made into a small theatre, with stage, auditorium, footlights, wings, and backcloth. Many years later we too acted plays there in what seemed to me a very Victorian little theatre, lit by oil lamps – its scene of 'Venice', its gold and white drawing room set, its woodland, still well preserved. Great pots of verbena, of hydrangea and camellia stood at the side of the orangery, under the glass roof, making a dark leafy background to the audience, many of whom were children of the earlier audience of 1866, who sat on gilt chairs in front and on benches covered with red baize further back. A thrilling emotion was evoked by the lighting of the footlights and by the drawing of the fringed red curtain, both to actors and audience.

The two periods merge together in my imagination, following one another like the movements of a Chopin 'Ballade' or 'Nocturne'.

Six

THE RECTOR OF LITTLE GADDESDEN

As at the end of winter, among the heaps of dead leaves upon the ground, one's eye falls upon a perfectly preserved lace-like leaf, a delicate memento of those green branches that once spread out in summertime, so my father's diaries, sketches and letters remind me of the skeleton leaves, like them, fragile and old yet preserving the form of his life, his mind, pursuits and person.

The writings are balanced and sensitive, the sketches full of zest, and the sermons, in spite of an old-fashioned theology, are manly and sincere. There are the compact little diaries, bound in red or black leather, and the small sketchbooks with their pencils attached that he carried in his pocket, sitting down on a bank or a wall to draw or jot down notes in a railway carriage. Or he might make caricatures at a cricket match, a clerical meeting or in a foreign restaurant or picture gallery.

The elder Lord Brownlow died at Mentone in 1867 of consumption, nursed by Lady Marion. Adelbert Cust succeeded to the title, and the year after he married my mother's beautiful cousin, Lady Adelaide Talbot, who has already appeared in these pages.

In 1870 my father returned to Little Gaddesden, this time as Rector, and it was to be his home till he died in 1892. Little Gaddesden Rectory was a comfortable square Regency house of brick with a grey slate roof. A short drive with a clipped yew hedge went up to the front door, which opened onto a stone-flagged hall with a balustraded staircase leading up to the landing above. The rooms were high and well proportioned and the windows looked out over Ashridge Park. There, across the Rectory field, one saw oaks and beeches growing out of undulating folds of ground, covered with bracken, part, it is said, of the primeval forest of England, never having been under the plough. Inside the park railings deer stepped delicately in and out of the glades, where the bracken grew high in summer, the sunlit sky shedding a blue sheen upon it, while, under the great trees themselves, whose grey trunks spring like masts without branch to right or left to leafy plume at the top, grew dark green moss, soft and moist in the shadow.

Every morning, when the family were at home, my father walked over to Ashridge to read prayers in the chapel, through these glades, with summer's thick tapestry and deep shadows in the dewy grass, or with winter sunshine slanting through the trunks, or mists rising from the valley. In spring there would be trembling green in countless buds on the beeches, or when again autumn frosts brought changes, bright yellow and brown fireworks of leaves burnt against a sapphire sky, and clouds of white, purple and grey.

Ashridge was a pleasant place with its own grandeur and its own beauty. The gardens shone with bright flowers, decked in Meredithian splendour. The house, a Gothic Revival structure designed by Wyatt, spreads out in a long line, grey and irregular. The garden stretches sedate and grandiose, with soft turf set with yew trees, ilex and rhododendron, and a fine avenue of lime along the south side. It was presided over by two tender-hearted aristocrats, brought up in the grand manner but humanised by thought and religion, who reigned for many years. The old photographs of the crinoline period show the company that suited it best to my mind, with the ample spread of each silken skirt brushing the Ashridge lawns, some ladies holding parasols, others with a foot raised and pointed on a croquet ball. Were the ladies aware of ignorance and starvation in the villages, or did they try to relieve suffering and want? No doubt they read of hard cases in the pages of Dickens, in Kingsley's *Alton Locke* or Mrs Gaskell's *Mary Barton*. Of course they knew of ragged schools and refuges, and visited hospitals. Victorian ladies were often surprisingly useful members of society, but their upbringing taught them to minister to distress rather than alter foundations and, as for ideas on the re-distribution of wealth, these were left to Radicals and Chartists.

My father worked constantly at painting and drawing and spent every spare hour taking notes in pencil and watercolour. In my mind his painting is interwoven with Hertfordshire landscape. His sketches from earliest childhood show the actual scenes in the neighbourhood of Little Gaddesden, the woodlands, farms, the fields and hedgerow, the Downs, streams and canals, the very skies, stormy or serene, and recall to me his paintings and his happy industry. How often, as I turned over the thick pages of the portfolios as a child, have the sketches seemed to lead me down actual roads, over real healthy commons, across arched

*Lord Brownlow of
Ashridge.*

canal bridges and through the beech trunks of Ashridge Park, where red
deer and fallow deer stood shyly at gaze, ready to spring away, flicking
their tails.

As rector, my father filled a role, not quite that of the country
parson, still less the sporting parson, nor the domestic chaplain of the
'Mr Collins' type; he was in many ways like Charles Kingsley, romantic,
full of life, and interested in each problem as it arose. For him both
Maurice and Kingsley, those ardent founders of the Christian Socialist
movement, Carlyle too, and Ruskin, were inspirations. He studied their
work and pondered over the solutions they offered for social problems.
Whether rich or poor, every man should have his rights. If carrying out
these principles in practice was not always easy, the artist in him helped
to bridge over difficulties; his eye took in details and made pictures
when he might otherwise have been troubled. He was never bored,
never contemptuous. From now on he gave many lectures to working
men on art, history and travel, following the principles of Frederick

Maurice who had founded the Working Men's College (with Ruskin, Tom Hughes, Burne-Jones, Rossetti and Vernon Lushington).

When visiting the people in his parish a laugh, a story, a reminiscence, stimulating new thoughts, would be more helpful than pious sentiment or even sympathy, though this too my father gave. In one diary is the entry: 'Sadness gives to earthly things a deeper richer-hearted tone, more valued on account of life's uncertainty.'

A story of my father in a friend's letter illustrates his character:

> On the verge of being involved in a quarrel with a rather pig-headed old gentlemen, who had totally misunderstood something I had written, I walked over to Gaddesden and laid the facts of the case before Lane. He simply roared with laughter over the other man's mistake and then gave me sound advice. 'Of course you are absolutely right and he is absolutely wrong. But as he is a much older man than you are, you can surely afford to give away a point or two and apologize – for what you have not done.' I did so and when, a week or two later, Lane met the old fellow, and explained matters to him, I in my turn received an ample apology and cordial invitation to dinner and we two disputants became staunch friends.

So at Little Gaddesden my father matured, and for thirty years belonged to the place, working at painting all the while. He knew everybody, drew portraits of labourers in smocks, old women in the Bede-house and children of the village. He would play cricket with the village team and some of his strokes were remembered with delight for years. He read the church services in the flint and stone church which stands on the edge of the long Dagnall valley overlooking the vale of Aylesbury. Perhaps his heart was not altogether in the church, and like many another his mind lingered in his studio. His sermons, scholarly in form, were practical and harmonious rather than original in thought. One of the notes which I have come across is the expression of a real love of nature, and runs,

> This beauteous procession from spring throughout summer. The snowdrop and crocus and then the wealth of lovely wild flowers, violets scenting the wayside, the yellow primrose and white constellation of anemones and hyacinths, as heavens upbreaking thro' the earth, we are all able to enjoy. The wild roses lighten up the hedges and the honeysuckle with its sweet perfume. This is the acted Parable of the Resurrection, the awaking and quickening of dead things to Life.

Random entries in diaries show his various interests:

> April 1878. Saw Millais. Val Prinsep nearly pushed the pot from the
> gallery which would have killed somebody. George Eliot there, not
> at all my idea of her – I mistook her for a kind old lady and very
> shy. G. Lewes a monkeyfied man. Preached on Christ's lament over
> Jerusalem – good congregation. Such a thunderstorm.

Here, at Little Gaddesden, he courted Caroline Boyle, niece to Lady
Marion Alsford's friend Mary Boyle, and they were married in 1871.
Hers was a docile, conscientious and deeply religious nature. Devoted
to one another, they lived a quiet life at Little Gaddesden Rectory. They
had two children, Adelaide and Margaret. In a book of quotations and
stories belonging to Caroline I find this description of a visit to an old
man:

> Dec 15. Not long ago, only a day or two before old Cox died, we
> went one snowy day to receive the Holy Communion with him. He
> was gradually passing away, and his voice was so weak that we could
> hardly understand what he said. Two or three times we tried to make
> out one sentence and at last we found out he was trying to say 'Be
> your feet wet, Ma'am?' At that last moment, when faint and weak and
> dying, he could still think of others with unselfish love.

Another shows her simple devotion to her husband:

> July 1878. I was very anxious when Charlton travelled all night long,
> rushing through the darkness, and carried away from me into the
> hollow of the night. I thought perhaps God would send a strong
> winged angel to fly all night before the train, to protect the one so
> precious to me.

When Caroline died in 1883 my father writes in his diary: 'Darling
Childie fell asleep'.

'I am always thinking of you,' writes Mary Boyle, 'It is indeed as if I
were with you. Rose writes me word of your beautiful sermon, and how
bravely you fought to obtain that calm which is such a poor substitute
for peace and yet is so desirable.'

The spring of 1885 he went abroad, with Ralph Sneyd, a favourite
pupil, to seek change of scene. At Lucerne he found 'colour of lake
superb, peacock's neck in hue, clear sky, much snow on mountains',
and next day 'had an interesting journey thro' St Gothard, waterfalls
full, Italian side lovely with fresh verdure of chestnuts'. At S. Croce in

Florence he met 'Duckworth and party of friends who were in Spain in 1868 – evening with them'; he was feeling more sociable again. He buys Ruskin's *Mornings in Florence* and notes how in the 'Giotto predella picture of the crucifixion, Christ lays his hand on soldier disrobing Him, as if to say – Do your duty, Be not afraid'. Later he notes:

> San Marco – the cloisters so very beautiful. The green and bright flowers in the centre – arcades decorated with frescos. Then the cells of the monks – well kept – the spirit of Savanarola and Fra Beato and Antonio. The Fra Beato pictures quite lovely. The beauty of the colour a revelation – blues of varied hues, and reds and whites, not often dark sombre colours. The 'dirt' school not yet arisen. Are the colours not an index of a serene and happy mind? The dark and sombre ones of a perplexed and doubtful mind? he asks himself.

On the way to Vallombrosa:

> ... up through lovely chestnut forests, pictures everywhere – streams, Etrurian shades of dark woods – arid hills higher – surprise at oasis of camoldol – comfortable drive to Bibiena on thro' woods to Lavernia by monks – one fat friar so polite and knowing – overcome by the beauty of the scenery, grand trees, birch and fir. Chapel of St Francis! Supper of herbs, spinach and omelet, Frati snuff much.

He gets letters from home and the diary goes on:

> How sadly the memory of my dear one comes to me! The morning at Lavernia 6 o'clock a.m. – birds singing, lizards playing, sunshine giving colour, the beauty of all this – the sense of loneliness – need her sweet mind. I could not make a sketch but only meditate ...

On his return home my father was offered the living of Berkhamsted, but he decided to stay at Little Gaddesden. Although the reasons he gives in his letters are connected with finance and the cost of a curate, one feels that his real reason was his love of Little Gaddesden and the park at Ashridge.

Life renewed itself for my father again and again; his 'luck' was in his own nature. Many a summer he went to stay in Scotland, sometimes as chaplain to people he knew, sometimes as an ordinary visitor. He enjoyed walking with the deer stalkers and ghillies, sometimes carrying a gun himself, though, as Lord Brownlow told me, he was never a very good shot. The rusty brown and purple of the hills, the rushing burns, the inlets of the sea, the gleams on the water and swift changes appealed

Charlton Lane in later life with W.G. Grace. The illustration is labelled '18 Veterans over fifty versus Gentlemen of M.C.C. at Lord's Cricket Ground, 16 June 1887'.

to his eye. The light evenings, the soft air of the West Coast brought out the colours he loved, dark and rich, in those rough surfaces of rock, the weather-beaten cottages, in the waves and ripples of water that he painted, all seemed subjects for pictures and their texture interesting to interpret in watercolour. Sometimes he drew an old piper or a ghillie and his dog, sometimes a stag, a waterfall, or a gnarled tree in his notebook.

In the summer of 1885 he went on the visit to the Brownlows at Applecross on the West Coast. Here he met Adela Talbot for the first time and then came a change in his life. He resolved to marry again. His romantic nature, now fully matured, flamed up in admiration for the tall young woman, who led a difficult life at home and was eager to learn about painting, poetry and philosophy. 'Mr Lane gave me a painting lesson', says Adela's diary. As the Withington letters show he did not win her at once. Staying at hospitable Brockhampton and sitting under some trees near the house, Adela wrote the letter accepting Charlton Lane, and then having done so she upset the ink pot over her gown! Into the house she rushed to report the accident and to remove the stains as best she could.

When she finally accepted him my father received a delighted letter from his old friend Lady Marion Alford.

> 3 Carlton House Terrace, 25 Oct. 1887
>
> Dear Mr Lane,
>
> You know how much I hoped that your hopes might be fulfilled. Now my prophecy that she was attainable has come true. I rejoice with you that you will have a home like a home once more.
>
> I am certain that the dear good woman you have won will grow in beauty of character every day. She has struggled bravely for culture all her life and has a noble disregard for the vanities of the world and trust for the realities of goodness.
>
> You must be very tender to her – but of this I have little doubt. I feel so sure that your dear first wife would have said 'do this' if she could have foreseen everything. I am sure her blessing will rest on any effort of Adela for her dear girls. At first I am glad she will be at Ashridge – so dear to Adela. Later I will hope that you may have promotion in the Church.
>
> Believe me dear Mr Lane Yours always sincerely, Marion Alford.

Charlton Lane came to Withington in 1887 and there he painted a watercolour of the prim grass-edged beds of geraniums and calceolarias, looking through the front door of the Rectory, showing the sundial in the middle and the belt of straggling trees beyond, shutting out the Cotswold valley. In the middle of the sketch is Adela's tall figure, and in the foreground, leaning against the front door is her father's spud, with which grandpapa used to dig up weeds, and sometimes more cherished roots as well. If the new admirer brought warmth and romance into Adela's life, he was helpful too in the vicissitudes of Withington, listening to the stories of poverty and illness in the village, engaging the new curate and making friends with other members of the family.

When Charlton asked her to marry him, Adela at first felt she could not leave Withington. The village, down whose street she had so often

Photograph taken on the occasion of the visit of His Majesty the Shah of Persia, Ashridge 9 July 1889.

walked, called her to remain, her father needed her, the very landscape seemed designed for her background; her mother was buried in the churchyard and her sister Emma, who had taken her for walks, had taught her how to live in childhood, to love music, trained her to face life and, too, to turn away from it. But Charlton wrote giving her a new turn to her thoughts:

> Dearest Adela,
>   I must write a line to you because I want to assure you particularly that I feel deeply with you about all your anxiety on the score of Withington duties – I am afraid you may think me selfish and inconsiderate and not able to see your point of view. Now it has been this very sympathy with your various troubles that has borne me up in the cloudy days – I cannot say how much I admire you for your right feelings – I want you to feel this strongly – that I am not

unworthy to share all your difficulties, however unworthy of you in other respects. You know I am not inexperienced in trouble, I have tried to learn some of the sweet uses of adversity that I may be able to console and strengthen others. I have found so often that there are duties which one has to leave to others and one does so at first in fear and trembling. Yes! This trial often has been present to me in life. I can only under such circumstances leave things in God's hands – pray to Him to find some fresh instrument to carry on one's work. It is a great trial of one's faith – God does His own work in ways that we do not expect, but does He not always reward us if we truly serve Him, wherever we are, by finding someone to act for us and for Him? It is I suppose in this vein that Milton wrote those grand words of his sonnet on his own blindness:

> Patience to that murmur soon replied
> Who best bear His mild yoke

> They serve Him best.
> Thousands at His bidding post
> O'er land and ocean without rest
> They also serve who only stand and wait.

In the change and chance of life our duties and offices must be left in God's hands – and in your case, my dearest, the very longing to fulfil them is truest prayer which must be answered by God. But be assured of my most sincere sympathy, the fruit of my true love for you, your very affectionate,

C.

Adela responds and accepts Charlton. A joyful letter comes from him, showing great sympathy with the things that were of importance to her but also concluding with an interesting note of his meetings with three famous men, Lowell, Henry James and Du Maurier; Lowell was to come into their lives again.

Aug. 12 1887

Dearest Adela,

Your blessed letter has made me immensely happy. Words fail to give any idea of my joyous surprise when upon opening the letter the first words which greeted my eyes were 'really your Adela' written in your tall 'fine Roman hand'. I had then such a rush of blood to the heart from over-joyousness – all your hesitation has only made you more and more valuable. I want you to know how much I admired your dear father – I thought him a fine specimen of high-born gentleman and his manner was so kind and courteous to me. I did not find it hard to make him understand me. I shall live henceforth to make you truly happy and show my appreciation of your goodness. I rejoice, moreover, that you will find many duties at Little Gaddesden.

He continues to follow Withington village life for the sake of his beloved:

Jan. 4th 1888

Dearest Adela,

Your description of the four poor dying folk is very touching; I hope they will die before you leave the parish. Remember me to any of them who value any kind word from me. The carrier interested me so much – he has a vein of humour ... Had a jolly walk in the park with three Wheatleys, who called to say pretty New Year things. A fine pathetic windy sunset, yellow bars behind rich maroon trees.

Darling one, goodnight – God bless you – I love to hear people talk with such admiration and love of you and then wonder at my having such a treasure.

Your loving,
C.L.

Jan. 9th

I got up to London this morning to find this place enveloped in thick fog. It is as yellow as a yellow old master. By the way, I was amused at a remark of Brewtnall, the artist, who said when he first went to live in the country he found the sunset 'too clean'. At Little Gaddesden the morning was superb – sun so bright and hot.

And again – just before his marriage to Adela:

Sweet face – modestly conscious of the affectionate interest of the congregation when the Banns are read. It is very good of you to stand – a Xtian martyr in the arena! I look forward to the 19th, to future peace and joy. May I be enabled to make you very happy.

As an engaged young lady Adela had begun to blossom; her diary grows a shade more sentimental when Mr 'Lane' is mentioned:

Ashridge, 2 July 1887

As we were finishing breakfast Margot Tennant arrived, having come to Euston in a milk cart. Adelaide, the Wharncliffes, Grahams and I drove to church in the break. On return wrote letters and then joined all the others sitting under the trees. Mr Lowell [James Russell Lowell] told some ghost stories. After luncheon the Charlie Beresfords arrived, and we took a turn in the garden. Then tea under the yews, and Addie photographed us. Some played lawn tennis and some went to the woods. The rose garden was lovely, and I sat there reading Browning. After dinner we all sat out in the moonlight all the evening. Mr Graham was singing when we returned. Sat on the terrace, then Mr Lowell, Mr Lane and I went to the other side of the moat and gathered heaps of ox-eyed daisies. It was 10.30 but the moon was very bright. We sat out till after 11.

That was as near the romantic as reserved Adela could get, but that evening's roaming made a poem for James Russell Lowell, and a year later he sent a copy of it with a letter to Adela:

The New Persephone

What power in Nature dwells that thus
Herself and Man she can restore,
And senses that long drooped in us
Make fresh and fragrant to the core?

New were the heavens, the stars were new,
And, in the amplitude of night,
Deep over deep of fleckless blue,
The moon was silent with delight.

Beneath the boughs the breezes slept,
The leaves were sound asleep as they,
And o'er the turf slow shadows crept,
Denser and drowsier than by day.

Fair Talbot spoke; the voice was low
And steeped in moonlight like the scene,
Yet summoned back from long ago
Of England's war the armoured sheen.

For in its ring I seem to hear
Softer vibrations of that lance
That cost the Sainted Maid so dear
And quenched the oriflamme of France.

'Come' said the voice, and on we went
Through grasses gray with moonlight dew,
To where in midnight's deep content
Fullblown the ox-eyed daisies grew.

How still and beautiful they were,
Those discs of unimpassioned snow,
Moored fast to earth, afloat in air!
How should their calm tease fancy so?

Like tiny moons they swim at ease,
And each, wide-eyed, its moonthirst slakes;
It was as when the goddess sees
Her image in a thousand lakes.

Still on our leader pushed to where
They thickened to a Milky Way;
At every step they seemed more fair,
More large and whiter than by day.

Dian leaned wondering from the blue,
Her ancient self she seemed to see
When with her nymphs, a lithe-limbed crew,
She tracked the glades of Arcady.

That step secure, that high-poised brow,
Almost to cheat me had sufficed,
But no Endymion waits me now,
Ungoddessed and astronomised!

A basket at her elbow swings:
Some new Persephone is this?
And of those two blackbreasted things
That follow her, can one be Dis?

The gloomy gods perchance are left,
Since science spares thee unbenign,
But me of mortal cares bereft
It wearies, banished here to shine.

Thus Dian to herself, or so
My fancy coined it word for word
And I 'gan feel myself de trop
A tête-à-tête's obtrusive third.

Our panier heaped, we homeward turn
Across the moon-contented field,
Then through the close where roses burn
Like those that reddened for Crimhield.

Some, basking in the moonlight, caught
Murmurs on song from Shiraz blown
And some, exiled in shadow, wrought
A fainter moonlight of their own.

And all the air with rosebreath flushed
As they, with passion red or pale,
Leaned forth and listened as if hushed
With descants of the nightingale.

Entranced amid the blooms we stood;
Looked we below or looked we above,
The world with all it held was good
And heaven and earth were full of love.

It seemed not night, it was not day,
Our hearts this atmosphere distil
As in the Land of Faraway
Which makes its weather as it will.

But the chimes jangle, 'You must go!'
And chiller grows the midnight's breath;
We are Time's puppets; high and low
Parts when he bids in life or death.

The sorcery fades from earth and air,
And from our feet the sense of wings,
The moon is but a lantern's flare
Lighting us back to common things.

O'er Ashridge's embattled walls
Ablaze with hospitable light,
A gray of sudden ageing falls
As we return to earth and night.

Long may its Lord and Dame control
This happy realm of field and hill,
And to the body and the soul
Of countless friends bid welcome still!

But ah, to me return no more
Such lunacies with such a guide,
For Dis was there and proudly bore
Away with him a happy bride.

The Brownlow's house at 3 Carlton House Terrace, from which my parents were married in 1888, was one of the imposing row to the right of the Duke of York's Steps overlooking St James' Park. The portico, the main staircase and the great rooms were on a grand scale, the basement remarkably dark and inconvenient. From the top storey windows one looked down on a mass of trees, the elms and planes of the Mall and St James' Park. Not far away were the pelicans and ducks, the irises and reeds by the water. Big Ben's strike reverberated slowly and tremendously and the twin towers of Westminster Abbey stood up against the sky and caught the light.

It was in this fine house of a more spacious age that Adela stayed for her wedding to Charlton Lane, and had the care and affection of her cousin, Adelaide Brownlow.

Seven

WIDOWHOOD: NETTLEDEN

Adela enjoyed the artist in C.G. Lane as well as the man of the world, one who could interpret her moods and the moods of nature, who through his painting could formulate 'the pathetic fallacy' that nature weeps and rejoices with human creatures. He shared with her a love of the poets, Shakespeare, Milton, Browning, Wordsworth and Tennyson. Here was an interpretation of her moods, here for both the value of life, beauty realised.

She was sensitive to beauty; the contemplation of a lovely flower or a bright bird brought her peace. If life for her was hard it was also exciting and absorbing, and so it remained to the end. The dark self-blaming days, the prayers for forgiveness, the feeling of failure threw into sharp relief the happy days when she was busily occupied, or when moments of breathless beauty came upon her, melodies that crept in on mind and ear.

To Adela a 'weltanschauung' without competition or strain seemed attractive and at times unattainable, an aspiration given 'a local habitation and a name' in church, in the 'peace of God which passeth all understanding', in the forms of worship and in hymns and the words of the Bible, as well as in poetry and music. Her husband gave her the confidence she lacked, and for four brief years she was a happy woman. Then came the tragedy, my father's death of pneumonia.

I was born at Little Gaddesden and so was my brother Tony. I just remember my father as he showed me a donkey in the field or made funny drawings for my amusement. I faintly remember being taken to say goodbye to him as he lay dying. Dimly I see a handsome whiskered man in a white nightshirt propped up in bed and myself being lifted up to kiss him. This was in November 1892. We children wore black and white pinafores after that for a time.

My mother was as if dazed. That autumn she had to gather up all the books and possessions my father had collected, her own wedding presents, his canvases, paint-brushes and palettes, and to leave the square and spacious Rectory. The question was where was she to live. A curious dread of being left homeless has always hung about me, perhaps a legacy of this early uprooting. Many people find moving easy, not so I. A cold wind seems to blow and shrivel up the leaves and flowers when a move has to be made.

My mother found a new home at Nettleden, only three miles from Little Gaddesden, one of the high-gabled vicarages built by Lady Marion Alford, now a vicarage no longer, standing on a hillside with a terraced garden, yew hedges and stone steps, a sunny place and, for children, a lovely one with its grassy banks, made for rolling and sliding down. Thyme grew in the short grass on the banks; its smell pervaded our happy tumblings and slidings from the yew hedge on the top to the lawn below. There were Irish yews at the base of the steps in imitation of the cypresses of Italian gardens, a rose-covered pergola framed a peaceful view of cornfields, woods and winding road shadowed by big elms.

The tiny village with its little grey church lay below, embedded in the trees, the smoke of the cottages turned to blue by the foliage behind. We knew all the villagers. When we went there straw plaiting was a home industry. The plaits went to Luton to be made up into hats. The women and children would stand in the doorways plaiting, giving a gay touch to the village.

For Adela, in her widowed existence, with two small children and the two Lane stepdaughters, there was often bitterness of heart and eating of humble pie, in spite of the sympathy and kindness of the Brownlows and all the Talbot cousins. Withington and its ways came back to her now she was alone; my grandmother's meticulous account books, the regular church-going, and the habit of visiting poor people: these duties once taken so lightly, and garlanded with simple thanks, now became a rule of life for her. So Adela took up her duties at Nettleden, her new home.

My own 'rectory' upbringing inculcated kindness and sympathy, a spartan attitude to comfort and a respect for authority, but it may have encouraged fatalism about illness. For my mother, though often too much taken up with writing letters and good works to attend much to us children and our fancies, would sit up with one of us when feverish and ill, fetch us books and toys, and this made going to bed the best way of getting out of boring tasks and being made much of. I remember having measles and my mother sitting in an armchair in the nursery. I cannot have been very old or very young either for I did a drawing of her asleep in the armchair. I was always drawing something or other: dogs, people, flowers, brownies, as children will.

Our gardens were at the bottom on the lowest terrace behind the high flint wall dividing our Nettleden garden from the village street. A many-stemmed hazel tree grew against the wall and hung over, and there, in its branches, we would sit, watching the road through the village and the few-and-far-between carts and carriages that passed. Sometimes in the afternoon, cousin Adelaide Brownlow would drive along in her low pony carriage flicking the cob with her whip with the tiny parasol half-way up it. As she saw us perched on the wall she would call out in her delightful bell-sounding voice, which was yet rather hoarse, 'You naughty children get down, get down', and shake the whip at us in pretended anger and we laughed. Opposite us, as we sat there, was the forge, and a constant sound of blows upon the anvil reached our ears. We could see Mr Gash, the blacksmith, in his leather apron, beating the molten iron into the shape of a horseshoe in the forge itself, or else fixing it on to the sizzling hoof of a carthorse, standing with his back to the horse and holding the animal's foot firmly between his knees. How familiar were the sounds of crunching of hay in the manger, the stamping of a hoof, the cries of the blacksmith, 'Keep still', 'Coop, coop, come on now', the hammer clicking in the nails and the rasp finishing off the job.

Nut trees and rhubarb grew against our wall and wild-growing currant bushes, whose juicy scarlet berries, acid sweet, were eaten by us and the birds, and growing along with them moss roses with pink wrinkled faces and sticky stems and leaves with clove-spicy smell, and the artichoke plants, grey, noble and classical (making me think of the acanthus leaf in my drawing copy) and the crown-like blue artichoke flowers.

All life, all wisdom seemed hidden in the smells and shadows, in the sunshine that brought out the perfume of the leaves, of the roses and the grass and that hatched out the little green beetle we called 'Midsummer Nights Dream'.

Sometimes there comes back to me the aching longing I felt to record the transient beauty. Painting and my father's watercolours showed the way to set about it. All the same the longing was for something unattainable. My mother would read poetry to us in a wood where she took us on Sunday afternoons. I remember trying, with childish effort, to draw a fallen tree with a bramble growing over it while she read Keats' 'Ode to the Nightingale' or Shelley's 'Hail to thee, blithe spirit' – I cannot remember which. At such times the sadness of beauty came over me and a hint of its timelessness.

Nettleden was once the home a poet, Mr G. Cautley, a friend of my father's, and hump-back like Pope, a cultivated man who had lived in Italy; 'Dovelike church upon thy nest' one of the poems began – my mother used to quote it. There was always talk of poetry at home, and I could not understand those who said they did not like poetry, and I was taken aback by the fierce partisanship I met later in poets. Poetry it seemed to me ought to be basic and grand and quiet, inducing peace rather than discord.

It is difficult to choose in the lumber room of childhood's memories; the scenes are too much mixed up. Looking on the world as a series of pictures, each with its own feelings, one did not see one's own circle as one among many nor did one visualise the age as a passing phase. I associate Ashridge with finding beech-nuts in the park as a child. The taste of them, the scrunch of dead beech leaves, and the smell of burning takes me back to the days when, soon after my father's death, my brother and I walked with our nurse on the slippery little brick path down into the Golden Valley, as that bit of the park is called, and up the other side at the end of which one came to the immensely long uneven front of the house, and the stone archway high above us, and some grown-up person would pull a curious loop-shaped bell, and after a considerable time one of the inner glass doors was thrown open by a footman and the big hall with high Gothic vaulting was before us. To the youthful senses the smell of the great house was hypnotic and alluring. In the conservatory was the sweet-scented plant with pink tassels called humia that one pulled bits off coming out of chapel after prayers, and orange trees in pots, and a marble fountain. The pseudo-Gothic chapel was light and pleasant, it had crimson-velvet tasselled cushions, and great leather-bound prayer books from the days of the Duke of Bridgewater, stamped with the coat of arms. The pews were in tiers, and we would file up into them, much as people get up into the choir stalls at Westminster Abbey.

A big house must have a lot of people in it to make it alive, and Ashridge when it was 'furnished with guests' was exciting. Going there was a constant joy to us; I cannot imagine my life without it. From five years old I remember the Ashridge smoking room, its smell of tobacco smoke and beeswax, its vase of peacock's feathers, its many pots from various countries, German beer mugs, Chinese ducks and Delft-ware standing on the polished ivory and ebony cabinet with spiral fluted pillars, the smoke going up into the chimney, a carved oak fireplace from some old house that had been pulled down, and, out of doors, the leaves racing in the wind.

In winter fiery splashes of sunset showed above the ordered tangle of tree tops. On the ground a chestnut-coloured layer of bracken topped slopes of grass, olive-green with streaks of snow in sudden whiteness, while towards sunset, grey rain clouds took on a greenish colour, and reflected a purple glow.

In the old days, when the great park was still untouched, one could wander on and on over the smooth grass, past clumps of big beech trees, and along the green drives. One of these led to Cox's, the head keeper's, a graceful Elizabethan house with the top storey jutting out; a split oak fence ran round the garden plot with its apple and currant bushes, outbuildings and kennels. A pond lay in front with a thick oak tree growing at one side. Rows of dead weasels, stoats and jays were nailed up on the fence. There was no road up to the house, only the smooth green grass, which gave the place a sylvan look and reminded one of the Forest of Arden.

The lime avenue was alive with bees in July, its immense trees holding myriads of them among its blossoms, the trees themselves so huge that human beings walking beneath them looked tiny. Seen between the boles, and bright in the sunshine, shone the flower beds of the Italian garden, held in squarely by crisp box hedges, backed by the spreading yew trees, set against the complicated unrestful outline of the grey stone house.

Every year the Flower Show happened at Ashridge, and then throngs of people walked through the gardens: relations, neighbours, village people, townspeople; they peered at the bright beds, at the solid waxy begonias, lobelia cardinalis, clustered phlox, red, pink and purple, the deep violet stars of clematis set round fine Italian stone vases, bright scarlet lychnis, heliotrope, plummy and sweet, fiery satin-white lilies and patterned Indian pinks. The verbena trees in pots came from Jamaica, and there was a magnolia on the law and agapanthus in pots.

In the round rose garden, surrounded by yew hedge and pillars, thickly flowering roses opened their soft petals, yellow, pink, crimson and white. How happy it made me to wander through from the smooth wide lawns and under ilex trees with their gnarled trunks and to thrust my face into the tender delicious roses in the circle. To childhood the effect of the garden was of a confused and magnificent beauty, bands of shadow and light, sharp smells of moist bushes, sunburnt grass and flowers. Near the rose garden was the rock garden of Roman pattern, with boulders of pudding stone, statues, hartstongue fern, bamboo and iris in the pools and a grotto, with a rough flint passage which smelt of damp. This was long enough to be quite dark at one place, and I remember as a child of four being chased down it screaming by a cousin, and very much frightened. Great trees were everywhere: Spanish chestnuts and walnut, that must have belonged to the old house and monastery, a Wellingtonia avenue that lacked beauty, and another of small close-growing beeches, that attained it. In July some bushes covered with tiny white roses used to delight me, the outer petals flushed with pink, the yellow stamens at the centre, and the endless number of upturned flower faces which seemed to me more than pleasure.

How we raced over the smooth lawns, exploring and recognising flowers, corners of the garden and scents when we drove over or came to stay. Running round from place to place in the immense garden was a great excitement in childhood, and well do I remember the smells of the different bushes and trees: the walnut, laurel, yew and lime. The Monks' Garden had a wall of flowers, giant sunflowers grew in the great border at the back, under gables, the latter a bit of Elizabethan work that remained of the old house, and in the middle was a fountain surround by ingenious heraldic devices made of clipped box and yew, the coats of arms of Brownlows, Custs and Talbots in topiary work.

On the stone terrace near the house sat or walked the dignified figures of our elders. Knowing we might be asked questions a little above our heads, we kept away in the distant part of the garden till tea time, exploring with other children and trying to keep our best clothes clean. From some far point on the green lawn we would see the great ones moving towards the tall French windows of the dining room and we knew tea was going forward. It did not take us long to reach the dining room where we shyly hesitated, wondering where to sit. The elect of the neighbourhood would be well away with the meal and the children would be drawn into some table or other – a buzz of talk filled the room with a civilised murmur.

Bundles of foxgloves often nodded in our pony cart, jogging along with the pony's trot as Nanny or Mother drove us home along the road. The glades seemed to stretch away endlessly. Bluebells came first, through deep light, more blue and more purple when the sun shone than one remembered, satisfying like a draught of wine, a soft heady perfume in the air, the little bells curled back on the straight sappy stems. Sometimes we rode and sometimes we walked through them. We had picnics at the tea house, a rough wooden chalet in the woods, to enjoy these woodland flowers. The Brownlows, the Alfred Talbots, the Neville Lytteltons all used to collect. Inside it was all wood, built like a Norwegian house, with a long table in the middle and rough Italian crockery on the shelves; we all sat round the big table and ate, the children with great eagerness.

Many picnics I remember, some when we boiled the kettle on a wood fire outside and some in the tea house itself. At one picnic the Neville Lytteltons brought their daughters Meesie and Hilda, and this gave us great satisfaction. Meesie (Mrs Charles Masterman) was supposed to be very absent minded and 'up in the clouds'; she had dark red hair. Hilda (Mrs Arthur Grenfell) was a lovely fair child. We played with the pools of water left in the cleft of a great beech tree, and ran about. Meesie and Hilda were dressed in pink cotton frocks, Hilda looking like the child in Sargent's 'Carnation Lily, Lily Rose' with her short hair, thick, ash-coloured and fair.

Lady Lyttelton wore a sailor straw hat with a black ribbon and a jaunty covert coat jacket with big revers; she rode a bicycle. Neville Lyttelton had a kind, wrinkled soldier's face; he wore a Zingari tie. I remember Lady Lyttelton pretending to crack an egg on Tony's head; it was supposed by us to be very funny. They lived in the summer at Stocks Cottage, half a mile below the tea house, and from there one got to it by walking down a steep chalky hillside. They were friends of the Humphrey Wards who inhabited 'Stocks', a fine Georgian house in the valley near Aldbury village. The Wards provided a good deal of interest and excitement, for they knew an endless number of 'clever' relations and friends. Mrs Humphrey Ward, with all her intellectual eminence, was most benevolent. She was, I gathered later, always engaged on a new novel besides carrying on good works, particularly for the London Settlement she was helping to found. Humphrey Ward was an art connoisseur, collector, and critic; they had many works of art in their house. It had a pleasantly intellectual tone about it. The Wards used to bring their guests to Ashridge for tea on Sundays. I remember Henry James coming with them one day and being buttonholed by Violet Cust with a flood of talk, somewhat to my mother's chagrin, for the author had been a friend of my father and during the tea visit had asked who my mother was. We went to Stocks for hockey matches; in one of these Clementine Hosier was playing, later to marry Winston Churchill.

All the expeditions involved driving in a dog cart, trundling along the white roads in a mood of expectation and excitement. The drive from Nettleden to Stocks was specially delightful, through the shades of Ashridge Park, down Aldbury hill with a view tremendously wide and lovely below one, far away trees tiny in the distance and showing up against a pinky band of sky on the horizon, and a chalky hillside and a chalk quarry to one side, Aldbury village at the bottom, the stocks, the old half-timbered houses, the pond, the church and then along the bottom on a leafy hedged road – then Stocks itself, the house standing behind a line of dignified lime trees.

On the tour of visits we took in summer that to Blickling was our favourite. My godmother, Constance, Lady Lothian lived alone in the wonderful Elizabethan house of red brick. It was approached down a straight drive with grass on either side, high yew hedges and symmetrical outbuildings, over a bridge of ornamental stone with a stone gryphon, and through a courtyard one had to enter. A dry moat filled in with smooth grass ran round the house; surprisingly ornate and grand was the main staircase with its carved figures and animals. I remember being at once thrilled and impressed by these figures and by the full-length portraits of George III and Queen Caroline in the hall. Cousin Concy Lothian had a wonderful aquiline nose and beautiful modelled forehead, and a somewhat tragic expression of face. She was the widow of Schomberg Lord Lothian, who had died as a young man, and before her marriage was Lady Constance Talbot. She wore a plain widow's dress of fine black merino and her whole appearance was of remarkable dignity and beauty. In a way we were made much of; it was a house now of ageing people, from Lady Lothian, who was much older than my mother, to John Burrows, the old coachman.

In summer we travelled about visiting relations, staying in country houses and at an occasional rectory. My mother was always animated when she got back to her own part of the world in Gloucestershire. At Cirencester we went to see a friend of my mother's, Alice Miligan, whose house was the best kind of spinster's abode, orderly, bright, sociable. I remember a trim little dining room and how after luncheon we crossed the sunny street and, going through a door in the wall opposite, entered the brightest garden I had ever seen. I can smell the flowers now and hear the bees buzzing. It was late August and in the beds were quantities of velvety salpiglossis like cups of wine, ruby-coloured, yellow, tawny, fiery red, dark purple and pink, splashed, streaked with colour, like a painter's palette, and the demure coronals of verbena, too, scarlet, purple and pink. I wandered about feeling happy and safe watching the summer butterflies alighting on the flowers (red admirals and peacocks), and there was a bright brown one whose name I have forgotten. Mother and Alice Miligan sat and talked. As I came near them I heard sentences, plans were being discussed and I learnt for the first time that I was to go to a day school. I was all ears – company! I loved it. Books, learning, games – I enjoyed them all. We were to stay at Hampton Court. It was a new opening and I was at a turn in my life.

School turned out to be very interesting and sociable. Hampton Court Palace seemed to me mysterious and vast, both the palace itself with its courtyards and passages and the great garden, which had special smells I remember still. Gemma Creighton, the youngest of Bishop Creighton's daughters, was my school-fellow and friend. The Creightons lived at the Palace and were a great source of interest to me, being more truly intellectual than anyone else I had met before. Their conversation at meals, and there were often a good many of them, was almost like a debating society at times, each one making a point and defending it with leisurely enthusiasm. Mrs Creighton seemed to be the chairman and was addressed by each speaker; 'but mother' they began, each in turn developing a separate theme.

Eight

MEMORIES

I remember the impression of neat well-shod feet, unaccustomed to hardship or work, going on the well-polished floors, on some 'kindness' or to admire some beauty in the garden or flower vase, to welcome a visitor; of dignified men and women sailing in to meals, ample and excellent ones, and then sauntering gently out again to drink coffee in the drawing room or ante-room; of these same people setting off on walks, dressed in cloaks and coats and accompanied by dogs. I had no great impression of reading, although people did read in their rooms, Harry Cust particularly, who told me he always read one and a half hours every morning. The brilliant Harry often stayed at Ashridge. He cannot be said to have fitted in entirely, he was too much of a hedonist for that; he often shocked people with his bold remarks and his Rabelaisian humour, but he certainly gave as much as he took. My mother did not quite approve of him, but at the same time she remarked once, 'Harry is always on the side of the angels.' There is no doubt he was one of the wittiest men of his time, with a mind apt and delightful, and a pulsating link with contemporary life, society and politics, journalism, and at the same time a certain affinity with the life of the countryside. No aspect of life left him cold.

Ease seemed the key note of Ashridge, not luxury, not self-indulgence, but the ease of the old aristocracy with its large outlay, its idiosyncratic servants, its great rooms. I see the big inner hall at Ashridge with its immense armchairs, its Della Robbia plaque, its large Nankin pots, in winter poinsettias grouped at the foot of the stairs, the red flowers standing out against the white walls. I see the ante-room, hung with crimson brocade, with gilt lines and scrolls on the walls, with a fine Dutch harbour scene by Cuyp, full of light, a Bassano, a so-called Rembrandt, a Van Dyck portrait and many other mellow and delightful works of the 17th-century schools. How rich they were. The well-washed

Morris chair covers gave a comfortable look to the high room, and the little painting of a dancing child by Lady Waterford on the table, the bunch of double violets or orchids and the silver magnifying glass gave it an intimate feeling. Through a pair of double doors, flanked with enormous many-coloured Chinese porcelain vases, one went into the dining room panelled in mahogany, with silver sconces on the walls and a row of square Italian Renaissance portraits round the top of the room and, hanging in the middle, a copy of Galileo's lamp. Many a scrap of half-understood intelligent conversation heard in childhood and youth in this room comes back to me. In those days when one followed but a few of the interwoven strands of talk, the voices, moods and characters of the speakers stood out all the more clearly to the youthful sense. Ashridge had the tradition of a great house with open doors and a generous culture of hospitality. Lord and Lady Brownlow together gave it an individual charm, a fragrance, a childlike quality. Her eagerness and love of goodness, combining with his happy nature, added something unusual to their tradition of English landowners and aristocrats. If she had enthusiasm and but little method, he on the contrary was neat-handed and orderly, but he lacked drive, as is often the case with sons of energetic mothers. He turned away from politics, great schemes, attending just enough to his own estates, to arranging houses and gardens to suit his taste, in London attending the House of Lords, and, in the country, shooting and entertaining his friends. He had the gift of enjoying things and making them interesting to other people: Reggie Talbot, aristocratic, almost austere, with a noble presence and little to say; Nina Cust, who had much learning hidden away, whose few words were spoken in low musical lisping tones and with a one-sided smile; the torrent of Ronald Storrs' stories, comments and jokes; Lady Brownlow's vague yet searching questions like 'What do you think about life?', her deep curiously genuine laugh; and Lord Brownlow's nervous gesture of tapping his broad chest with a fine square-fingered hand as he listed to or told a story, and his stag-like movement of the head.

Mrs Watts would come to stay, a prop of the Home Arts and Industries Association, herself a craftswoman and an artist, dowdy but distinguished, a Fraser Tytler of Aldcurie, clear spoken, intense, with a deep incisive manner, quiet and held in, a pretty face like a faded rose leaf, small-featured and grey-eyed. She used to wear little bonnets with a ruche inside next to her face and old-fashioned picturesque clothes, very neat and rather like Kate Greenaway.

The large scale of Ashridge sometimes seemed overpowering to the young, but usually or mostly, to me as an artist, there was beauty to be found and much interest in the people.

Margaret Talbot was a Stuart Wortley, tall and remarkably handsome, with an upright slender figure, an intellectual and proud face not without austerity. Sapphire-blue eyes looked sometimes kindly, sometimes coldly from that countenance, long and narrow, the eyebrows arched, and the mouth straight and passionless. Her clothes were in the best taste, plain and perfect; one felt much 'education' about, and she was a member of a large family of brothers and sisters, none of them easily pleased. Some people thought her worldly, but I am inclined to think she accepted the values of her class and set, that she had learnt an austere religion from her mother, and had absorbed a great love of beauty and the arts from her brothers and sisters in youth – all these elements she combined in a grand fashion, though sometimes showing an almost childish respect for one of these values. The religious people and the dowdy found her worldly, but the 'mondains' found her intellectual and aloof. The music she so loved gave her balance, and perhaps her native humour as well helped to give her a particular sanity.

Violet Cust was amusing, warm-hearted, with a vast flow of talk and insatiable interest in people, whose every turn of phrase contained an allusion or quotation, exceedingly apt, illuminating and humorous. Her life was lived between the house of relations and the London flat, know to us all as 'flatty', where there were pretty things coming from various houses belonging to the past: old china, portraits, Arundel prints, sketches of the family houses, each calling up some association. The shrill voice, the flow of questions, the stiff little forefinger laid firmly upon one's arm to emphasise a point or insist upon an answer to one of her questions, the small plump figure, with the little blob of nose and almost comical face, the eyebrows well raised to denote pathos, and in speech the old-fashioned precision of expression often used for telling the most rakish stories, and a quickness which could never let its possessed be out of date: such was Violet Cust, 'Aunt V' to so many.

Gertrude (Geity), Lady Pembroke, was by then a strange imposing figure with a wild look in her eye and a fantastic nature. Her voice was instinct with character and her remarks curiously penetrating; she was singular and erratic but immensely dignified. She would walk slowly through the drawing room at No.7 Carlton House Terrace dressed in a gown of black lace, with erect bearing, turning her body but never her head to look at anything, tapping her front teeth with her fingers; she was strange but not sinister. A wealth of feeling, the vague, unexpressed feeling of a vast family circle, the picturesqueness of her Irish mother, so good and so erratic (in the Beresford tradition), and of the grand manner in which they had all lived, combined in her with a touch of caprice, a 'childishness' faintly reminiscent of Lady Caroline Lamb.

If in summer we travelled about paying visits, in autumn we had lessons with a governess, till my brother went to school, and the Christmas holidays we spent at home. I remember the Alfred Talbot's Christmas tree from nursery days, a real family affair. We drove over in the pony carriage, up the drive in the darkening afternoon, my mother, and us two children, driven by our coachman in his countrified livery. The porch door of Little Gaddesden House had fairy lights round it and the door was opened by the old butler with side whiskers. The long passage with is painted walls and inlaid furniture, its giant chrysanthemums and evergreen wreaths, looked grand and partified. I wore party shoes and a party dress, with hair carefully brushed, and Tony had on his new tie. Round the tree, when we entered the dining room, were familiar faces, all smiling. Most of the men were tall, our host Cousin Alfred Talbot handsome and benign with a little grey beard; he always wore spats and a buttonhole, violets or a white carnation. Cousin Emily, the hostess, moved about bouncingly among the guests, hospitable and gay, attired in an Elizabethan fashion in a dark dress with slashed sleeves and jewels. The Brownlows would be there, revolving among the lesser fry. There would be the plump figures of Mr Tomlinson, an old friend of the family with a frog-like countenance, and of Miss Evelyn Noyes, the great talker of the village. Etty Wheatley, whose enigmatic, lively Cust repartee made her a little alarming; her witty sister Violet Cust and her husband Nep Wheatley, the Ashridge agent, with his kind, thin, old soldier's face; and sometimes the mysterious and beautiful Nina Cust as well, her white face framed in fur and on it a spray of bay pinned with a turquoise brooch: all these I see against a background of dark blue curtains. A strong smell of burning fir branches mixed with the flower scents, and the flickering light of the candles with the shining of silver ribbons and brighties on the tree. We children wandered about and peeped at the parcels, neatly wrapped up and tied with ribbon, round the shining tree, while the elders greeted each other and talked in the grown-up way over our heads. The presents were handed round, and beautiful ones the were; someone's gift might be a book, like the one on lettering given to me one year which I looked at day after day and year after year with absorbed interest. I never know which I enjoyed most, the hum of conversation round the tree, tea time with the cousins or driving home down the drive with the fairy lights on either side of it, we children well muffled up and sitting on the back seat of the pony carriage, the carriage lamps flashing on each tree trunk along the road; and before going to bed there was the excitement of looking at the presents all over again.

At home in winter Tony and I spent delightful days in the stableyard, helping to groom the cob, or chopping wood with the garden boy or cleaning the knives or our own boots and shoes; the smell of boot and knife polish had its own potent charm in those days. Or we would clean out the rabbit hutches, which smelt less sweet, and watch the soft furred rabbit looking out with its round bright eye and its twitching whiskers. I cannot describe the joy of playing about in yard or in garden at home, looking at everything that grew: rhubarb shoots pushing up, twisted ivy with shining pointed leaves, bare oak branches with brown buds, yellow jasmine making little stars in winter, daphne myzereon, a cluster of tiny purple flowers wonderfully sweet-smelling, or Christmas roses white and veined with green and streaked with purple, sturdy and delicate, their flowers like candid faces opening to the winter sky. I thought the pump had specially pretty ivy, growing round its stone trough, and overhung by hazel bushes – the first to show yellow lambstails blowing about in February and March winds. Little curled leaves of cow parsley began to show above the ground in February and aconites opened their greenish yellow cups to the sun; snowdrops hung their four-fold cups out – white bells, growing in clumps in the orchard, strong and pushing up the faint fresh smell of early spring. There were so many of them I fancied I could hear their white bells ringing as they shook in the wind.

When we were still quite small my uncle Gustavus and his family came back from Ceylon and took a house at Harpenden in Hertfordshire. These cousins seemed to belong to us in a special way and made an exciting element in our lives. Cecil, the eldest girl had the gift of making all of us children contented and fair, though she kept the spirit of adventure going. Reggie, the sailor, was looked up to, while Conty, Gar, and Humfrey, the ones who had lived all their short lives in Ceylon, made an amusing, contentious trio. We grew up as a party of cousins. The Harpenden house was not like my home at Nettleden; there was more life, more noise and more variety. My aunt and uncle held to many Withington ways but had had the 'come and go' of Ceylon life, and the gaiety perhaps came from that. My uncle read family prayers, and everyone went to church on Sundays; guests came to stay and all the bedrooms were generally full. Furniture had been put in helter-skelter, from Withington, eked out with odds and ends. It was comfortable and pleasant. As time went on they moved to Marchmont near my home, an 18th-century house near the high road with a delightful river flowing through its fields, an avenue, and some big trees planted in bosky groves. No wonder my uncle liked it; there was something of Withington Rectory about it, though it was a real Hertfordshire house.

At this Harpenden house we celebrated New Year's Eve, for some reason called 'Jasper Tree Night' (possibly from the jewels in the Book of Revelation read in church, sardonyx and jasper). To mark the occasion we children dressed and had dinner with the grown-ups and danced among ourselves; we thought it all thrilling. Conty played the piano and we others sat in couples under a large chrysanthemum in a pot, a sort of cosy corner such as there used to be in the drawing rooms of those days. This was the 'jasper tree' so named by Humfrey, who had the faculty for making absurd things exciting; perhaps his large blue eyes had something to do with it, or was it his funny little nose, or the way he played the fool and made jokes? The long low dining room with a beam in the ceiling and a red wallpaper and red plush curtains, when the candles were lit under red shades, looked warm and old-fashioned, and there were raisins and almonds on the table, and home-made biscuits, a pot of ginger, guava jelly from Ceylon. *Alice in Wonderland* was our reading at Christmas, read by Conty in the schoolroom. We knew it by heart and quoted it as slogans during our games of family hockey.

My mother was rather shocked at the songs we sang and at the pickles and other unsuitable food the children were allowed to eat, and noise and jokes generally; but still we always went to stay each year and things went well, and we did not give her much trouble.

One Christmas holidays I especially remember. By this time some of the cousins were grown up; Cecil was married, Reggie was generally at sea, and Conty a romantic young lady. The two younger boys had left school and Humfrey the youngest was cramming for the army. My brother Tony had grown very tall and was at Winchester. He and I still enjoyed our times with 'the Gussies' as we called them. One winter's day we had cherry brandy when all the puddles were frozen and the pond by Sharman's Mill was covered with grey ice. Skating round it I saw the surrounding slopes of the shallow valley from new angles, the bushes standing up stiffly against the frosty fields; I was beginning to see landscape with the painter's eye. There was much screaming and laughing before we finally separated, my brother and I taking the rough lane past the farm's low buildings by the *Red Lion Inn* with its red curtains, and along the road, frosty and bright, home to Nettleden, to find my mother in the very low big chair of dull blue, with piles of parish magazines and copies of *The Times*, books of poetry and biography beside her. It was always the same, a small fire burning in the grate, some evergreen branches in a copper pot. It was a pretty room and a comfortable one. Everything there spoke of the past, and of the three rectories that went before.

Pictures of Nettleden crowd back to me. The nicotiana and the moon on the terrace; Mother and Tony and I walked up and down as the bright electrical moonbeams' white light flooded the world, the garden, the cornfields, the village roofs below. It was September, how precious; the holidays would soon be over and we enjoyed them so much. The voices of my mother and brother were pleasant and low; my mother enjoyed her son's company and savoured his time at home to the full. It all fell in with her emotional nature and her sociability.

Hunting started in November. Hunting – dewdrops, bright shining points, mist blown towards one; small twigs of hazel and beech outlined against the fog. Broad shapes, shoulders, hats, legs outstretched on saddles, horses' rumps, crackling through branches. Fern and bracken, erect and crisp, spread over the open spaces; blackberry leaves, red, purple, yellow and green. Toadstools are over. Spruce is furry, moss is green, tree trunks glisten and sweat, lichen comes to life in tiny grey cups; oak leaves, crenellated, are still on the branches, leather-coloured. Ash is all fallen and hazel is getting catkins, tiny absurd fingers; gorse, freckled and sharp, catches in horses' flanks and gives a tiny prick which draws blood. The close-clipped haunches of the well-groomed animals feel it the most. Clanking they go over the posts and rails. The men on their backs are like them, well-groomed, moving rhythmically in the saddle, their black or pink coats, white buckskin or drab cord breeches fitting them nearly as well as the shining skins of the horses.

November was the time for sharp-smelling tight-bunched marigolds in the garden, for violets to be picked, winter violets that pushed up under brown nut leaves and between bright blades of grass. All these grew at the bottom of Nettleden garden, in the part once cottage garden and now nearly all orchard. Governesses, German and French lessons in the autumn; music lessons, scales and finger exercises. Mother playing Chopin or Beethoven rather heavily but rhythmically upon the piano.

In contrast to this life were the short visits to London, generally during the 'Season'. This was the London of the *Merry Widow*, and Strauss' waltzes with their springing rhythm. People smiled as they danced. There were slow waltzes with long steps, the long white gloves we wore to the elbow, and 'Princess' dresses; our hair was done in little curls heaped high or kept in place by a Grecian wreath of gold leaves or perhaps a graceful wave on the forehead. Carnations were a favourite bouquet. There were butterflies and wallflowers then as now; I do not remember being quite one or the other, for I had some lovely dances, as a rule, but seem to remember sitting out and watching some of them, which I rather enjoyed. A friend once said, 'It's fun taking you to a dance, you always look so happy all the time.' Talk was, perhaps, a little stilted and I was overjoyed when someone would talk about Turner's paintings or Plato. One fascinating tall Hungarian and I made great friends over Plato and I always fancied the only anonymous gift I ever had, an attaché case, must have come from him. He had much to say about the plains of Hungary and the splendid horses there were to ride, but then he was a rich young diplomat. Had I carried too many small parcels to a smart luncheon party when we met, and left them in the hall?

One heard a good deal about the 'wrong people' getting into society, but there seemed plenty of the right ones to go on with, and didn't they know it! Some of the right ones were quite poor and took rooms in Ebury Street for three or four weeks. But I think mothers and daughters enjoyed themselves and fathers too, parading the Park on Sundays after tea and meeting their old friends, the elm trees just in green leaf, throwing becoming shadows over old and young, on toppers and feather boas and muslin flounces and picture hats.

At 19 I went to the Slade School. It was my third art school and was three times more interesting to me than the others. Sir Hugh Lane, whom I knew through the Lytteltons, gave me an introduction to Prof. Tonks, who ruled at the Slade in all his later glory. I have had no cause to question his supremacy for I found him a fine teacher and a delightful person. Against the greys and dirty greens of the wall of the 'art rooms' I see him advancing in a grey suit, tall and bony, the upper part of his face eagle-like, the lower part having a slightly long-suffering and amused look, as of an observer. His autocratic manner did not alarm me and his disquisitions on drawing given to Edith Phillips and myself, both new students, really did open my eyes and describe a method.

Pinafored girl students moved about the passages and classrooms, a smell of oil paint pervaded everywhere, and robust male students lounged and argued. Happy times. Every face and character seemed to stand out against the olive-green paint and grey stone of the Slade. It was a world of its own with Prof. Brown the head, Tonks, Russell, Child the secretary, and Lees the youngest member of the staff, not to speak of Steer who taught painting. The life drawing I always enjoyed, though I was never a star pupil; Tonks' lessons on figure drawing are what I remember best, his citations of Ingres and the old masters and his intense interest in structure.

My evenings were spent among relations, for I was usually staying at 12 Manchester Square, with the Reggie Talbots. Their house was well appointed in every way and they often entertained remarkable people, most of whom were connected in some way with Government service. Although properly impressed with empire builders and persons of high degree, I was generally too tired and sleepy after a day's work at the Slade to enter into another and an older world. Still it made interesting contrasts. The main problem seemed to be getting clean in time for dinner! Whether to be dirty and punctual or clean and late – I am sorry to say I generally chose the latter! Cousin Margaret was both kind and alarming; she was not easily shocked or bored though she had a great idea of living to a plan, so was apt to cut short one's conversational rambles. I fancy she found the Talbot mentality a little formless, though she had an affection for the family. Her father, James Stuart Wortley, was a Parliamentary lawyer, and no doubt she had learnt from him to form clear judgements. Her husband was soldierly almost to a fault, but with a Talbot twinkle and love of innocent leg-pulling and exceedingly kind-hearted. She had what was known as 'the Wortley manner', which meant putting people right, but in what I thought rather a charming way. I think I enjoyed being corrected on the whole and for this preceptor I had a great devotion. Having lived abroad, both in Paris as wife of the British Military attaché, and in Egypt, her views were not parochial; she had read a great deal, both in French and English, and she was a fine musician. There was a sympathy between us and on the whole she helped me to clear up my ideas.

These were still the days of good servants and the Reggies' butler, Mr Fripp, was a byword. His head was a shiny ostrich egg, his manner a blend of faithfulness, observation and pomposity. He adored his masters and they him, and any domestic who worked under him knew the true ritual of the dining room. To me he was ever kind and fatherly and when I was given what Cousin Margaret called 'cat's meat', or a small meal on a tray, it was brought up by Fripp, punctual and beautifully arranged. I liked these meals when my elders were out, when I could read the books from the shelves and write letters on their almost regal notepaper.

Nine

LONDON: THE SITWELLS

I wish I had kept a diary of the days when Edith Sitwell first came to stay with us. I went to meet her at Berkhamsted station, and driving up the hill on to the common in a one-horse fly Edith said, 'Are you keen on poetry?' A tall slender figure, stepping on long narrow feet, she had a curiously distinguished and enigmatic air. She wore a floppy hat and pale suede gloves. Soon after her arrival she brought sheets of music down to our drawing room and played, exceedingly well, Chopin, Brahms and Debussy. It was early summer and we used to wander about the fields and watch the wind brushing across the tops of the young barley, and as it whitened the field in waves Edith said, 'It's as if these are all the people who will come into one's life.'

I did drawings of her in my studio. We sat on the lawn by a privet hedge and Edith read Swinburne. Conty Talbot, my cousin, would drive over in a dog cart, in a blue linen frock, and sit in the drawing room playing with her beads and listening to Edith's music.

But soon we all moved to London, to a house in Sloane Court Sir George Sitwell, Edith's father, had taken for us for the London season. We were serious pleasure-seekers, Edith and I, Edith reading poetry, Swinburne, Verlaine and Baudelaire, and practising Brahms, and I going to art school in Chelsea where John and Orpen taught and more often Mr and Mrs McEvoy. Sometimes one of our relations gave a party to which we went, Edith dressed in white brocade with golden lily woven in it. She generally looked aloof and amused. It might be a musical party at which the fellow guests were not as serious about the music as we could have wished – 'Philistines', Edith called them; I suppose they were.

Our house was next door to Lord Monteagle's and we came to know his son, Tom Spring-Rice, the most ardent of musicians. We heard him practising the piano sometimes, before he went to the Foreign Office. Sometimes he came to dinner and played to us; I remember Brahms'

Variations on a Theme by Handel, beautifully played; we greatly enjoyed those evenings. And sometimes Edith's naturalist cousin Reginald Farrer came and entertained us with his curious humour. Occasionally we went to dances, but I have no distinct memory of them. As a hostess my mother was a mixture of nervousness and ready wit; our dinner parties confused me sometimes. We all wore very long full dresses in those days, which 'did up' at the back. Mother wore black and Edith pale green or white, and I had a pink satin dress with a draped corsage.

I see the hot street out of the window of Sloane Court in the morning and Tom Spring-Rice walking quickly down his front steps, clasping a F.O. despatch case and an umbrella and hurrying away in the direction of Whitehall. Then a policeman on his beat, then a drunken woman with a mottled face, swaying uncomfortably and looking out of place in this respectable neighbourhood, removed by the policeman, then the butcher's boy and the maids coming up the areas. Indoors there would be boxes of flowers from home, rather humble ones, columbine, dull red and blue, ox-eye daisies and iris, purple, white and yellow; these had to be put in water, and while I did this Edith would wander about and beg me to do the cockney imitations that amused her so much. She was always ready to laugh at one's most feeble jokes.

Almost next door was the rather Londony family of a pretty schoolfriend of mine, with a tall good-looking brother and a father and mother who made me rather shy, and a small brother in sailor suits. Edith was an enigma to them. 'Why does she always read Swinburne? Is she in love?' they said.

Even Lord's cricket ground saw Edith dreamily walking round with the crowd of us, dressed in pale green with a white feather boa flying out. We found a good many cousins and friends in that vast inconsequent crowd, but I doubt if anyone was ever less interested in cricket than Edith! Our outings to see her brothers at school were the greatest fun. Osbert was at Eton, and in his room we had solemn colloquies, with obscure Sitwell jokes about people I did not know. We strolled, the three of us, about the streets and round the schoolyard abstractedly.

Sacheverell was a fat little schoolboy with brown eyes and a very soft voice. He was at a private school at Reigate. He adored his sister and she him. Edith always produced jokes and evoked strange situations; she was a delightful companion. There was a softness and poignant sympathy in her as well as the strong personal prejudice that sharpened her angle of vision. She always seemed harmonious with

Osbert and Sachie. Edith wanted to see everything in a new way. My rectory outlook must have seemed mild and humdrum compared with her baroque worldly one; she said I was only interested in ploughed fields and porridge. Her beautiful speaking voice and her silky laugh always charmed me. The eccentricity of her parents, Sir George and Lady Ida, her travels taken in the grand manner, her knowledge of French literature made her at once more at home in the world and more suspicious of it than I.

She found herself misunderstood; her tastes were in those days applauded very half-heartedly at home. Detached alike from her relations and all of us she preferred her two brothers.

When I went to stay at Renishaw I saw the background that explained her. The house itself, long, battlemented and brooding, the beautiful terraced garden sloping to the valley below, the Italian fountains and terraces made a strong contrast to its setting, a coal-mining country with blast furnaces that flared up at night. The house was haunted. Inside, it had a solemn luxury about it, but the great ballroom was full of light and held it like a bubble between the high ceiling and the polished parquet floor. Large pieces of Italian and French furniture were beautifully placed in that room. I remember their shadows reflected in the parquet floor; a fine Sargent family group hung up at one end.

Edith, in white, swaying slightly, played sometimes Scarlatti and Corelli (to please me), or Brahms and Debussy to please herself, the Indian queens and Roman captains of the tapestries seeming part of the music with the avenues and garlands of flowers surrounding them. Sir George was a master of landscape gardening. Renishaw flowers were mostly white or mauve – white phlox, snapdragon, gladiolus, melting into the distance. Statues gleamed faintly, standing on either side of the steps that led down the middle of the garden. Dreamily we wandered over the lawns and along the paths, the boys flicking pale blue Eton handkerchiefs, and down to the lake below, or rowed about in the boat. Sir George arranged games of tennis, which he thought good for us; neither he nor Edith seemed made for the game – she played most unwillingly. The note of sadness seemed more the *malade du siècle* than the awareness that the times were out of joint, to which we were later to become accustomed.

Ten

INDIA

Strange to say, it was when I went to India with Conty and Willy Sitwell that I missed my home, though the new scenes and people delighted me. I had been to Italy but never so far before. At Bombay I 'met up' with the Sitwells, who had gone out by trooper. As we drove along the streets the first evening we saw a board over a house saying 'Home for Indigent Zoroastrians' – to think sun-worshippers could be indigent; but really it was just a home for poor Parsees.

Next day we started on the journey to Quetta; this entailed a journey on a B.I. boat to Karachi, up the coast, and then the day and night train journey. Not knowing Willy Sitwell well I was a trifle over-awed by this grey-haired soldier. But when I found that he gave zest to whatever we all did, I became devoted to him. He was interested in India and central Asian life to an unusual degree and showed Conty and me a great deal.

Willy enjoyed Conty's and my delight over the landscape, as we travelled through Sind, witnessing the patriarchal scenes of the family camel at the railway station, on which husband and wife mounted, both dressed in the baggy trousers, the man with a pink coat and a faded blue turban, perhaps, and the woman with coin ornaments, to be carried away by the mincing step of the camel towards jagged hills – the curious plumed bushes and camp fires in the dark. Willy knew Afghanistan in his youth and could point to Afghan and Persian influences everywhere. He knew the Indian Army, he understood the age-long Hindu-Musulman difference; he admired all the fighting races and mountain peoples. As we got into the hills we saw large flocks of sheep, black and white, 'ringed and straked', coming down the valley driven by shepherds to the plains for the cold weather, whole families accompanying them. We were delighted with the shepherds' clothes, their caps and the Afghan trousers, coat of black or white felt and the tents of red or black that were set up for the night. The hills here are of rock and for part of the day take on the mauve colour of hills in Persian miniatures. Quetta itself, surrounded by these hills, proved to be a largely military station with bungalows, cantonments and a native city and markets. The three of us were ready to get the most out of it, all in our various ways. Willy declared Conty revived at the sight of colour and that he could cure her of tiredness by taking her for a drive in the native city, and he took me for rides across the plain between the hills, beside the green crops, across the little irrigation channels, past rows of chenar, the plane-like tree whose leaves appear in the Persian miniatures, willows and apricots. We met riders, who came, as it seemed, from the Persian pictures too, in tight jackets and baggy trousers, turbaned, with turned-up shoes, but nobody bore arms except the British Army. We went out hunting, chasing the jackal, jumping nullabs alarmingly deep and galloping over the bright green crops, Willy in a white topee, grey or white breeches, and a tweed coat. The Quetta Hunt had much to recommend it and went well. I enjoyed the meetings out hunting best, on the whole, more than those at the club or at dances; the famous club seemed stuffy and impersonal.

The life of Quetta was complete in itself and had history and tradition and, of course, reminded one of Kipling's stories. One heard names of famous Indian regiments like Hodson's Horse. The British officers of these Indian regiments all spoke several native languages and naturally spent many years in the country. They were generally polo players and rode to hounds and in point-to-points, knowing all about horses, walers from Australia, country-breds and Arabs. Living in and out of stables, where Indian syces and grasscutters looked after the animals, they seemed to share the ponies' and horses' lives even more than do horse-lovers in England. One such was a tall Scotsman, whom I made friends with; he was a whipper-in to the hunt. He had a 16-hand animal that he persuaded me to ride astride and the creature bolted with me when we got to the open ground where he was accustomed to having his head; but I did not come off. At the end of the hills the horse slowed down and I was still in the saddle; my friend was a little concerned and I explained that I was more accustomed to riding side-saddle. We rode home more quietly and he gave me tea in a bare comfortless bungalow, which seemed full of bridles and bits. I was shy, and a bit shaken probably by the ride. I believe he was considering me as a possible wife, so it was reported by Mrs X. Accustomed to the frills of life, culture, and small talk I felt ill at ease with the strongly masculine atmosphere of that house and its stable smell

– and yet I liked it and its master, and keep an impression of something genuine and strong. Time has taught me, perhaps too late, that to feel is one thing and to interpret one's feelings another.

Quetta in spring, on my return there, was beautiful, its fruit trees in blossom against the bare mauve hills, its willows and poplars, golden-yellow in young leaf. Conty and I found hyacinths growing singly in the grass of the race course and exquisite tiny tulips, striped pink and white. Often we went in the tonga to paint in the country. Anne, Conty's child, had come out from England, a curly-headed baby of two, with Baba, the old Ceylon nurse. It was pretty to see Willy Sitwell play with her, the most adoring of fathers – Anne's rather serious baby face with round cheeks and pointed chin opposite the weather-beaten regular features of the soldier, eyes and mouth puckered with smiles and laughter for the little daughter: 'My little piece' he called her. Willy as brigadier wore dark blue uniform and a white topee on Sunday, and he read the lessons in the big garrison church. The smell of a soldier congregation is different from other congregations.

The fruit trees were still in flower, the prickly little apricot, and the pink peach, when I had to pack to go home. The peculiar smell of the big trunk's inside, of gum and calico, was wafted toward me as I put in the riding boots, the coat, the sketch books and the few lengths of bright silk I had bought, and the embroidered marriage quilt of Sind.

I left Quetta one afternoon by the train that went down the Bolan Pass. The little commonplace railway station was full of topees; a good many people seemed to be leaving. As their train steamed off, the little group got smaller and smaller and the rocky hills resumed their original importance in the landscape – eagles wheeled in the sky and kites and vultures perched on the scattered trees. After this memory becomes blurred in a disastrous visit to Nettleden; a visit to Ashridge, and then comes August 1914 and the War.

Almost anything looks picturesque in retrospect, probably because it is now fair game for a work of art or a theory.

Eleven

1914

When war broke out in 1914 my mother and I were staying at Ashridge in all its summer pomp. Autumn saw London Territorials camped around us at Nettleden. One or two of the younger ones would come to our house for music. Our drawing room, with its Morris wallpaper, Empire chairs and big curly mirror, seemed a good background for music. In all of us burnt the spirit of music, part-singing and playing the piano, though the performances were humble enough. The young soldier I remember best was very tall; he had a small fair head and blue eyes and looked rather childlike, in spite of his small moustache. He spoke with a pleasant voice in disjointed sentences and laughed a great deal; we knew many of his relations. He used to ride over to see us on a big horse of which he was very proud; I remember the creaking of his leather equipment and smell of leather leggings. The atmosphere of a religious home hung about him and at the same time he had a touch of the great world. He had a very sweet tenor voice and musical sense. As autumn turned to winter, then to spring, we practised duets together and sang them at camp concert in the rough tent at the farm by the river, near which lay watercress beds like green frills on the surface of the water. Outside the horses could be heard stamping in their stables. Inside, by the flickering light of lamps, were the tommies in rough khaki tunics with bright buttons, thick Army boots, and their caps with stiff round tops pushed under benches. The tent was a dingy grey canvas; it was full of smoke and the cockney voices sounded like so many birds chattering and whistling. It all seemed very out of the way and countrified.

We sang Mendelssohn duets not untunefully, he standing upright in khaki, and I reaching up to share the music, dressed in a fur cap and coat with a grey fur collar.

It was early spring. Soon I was to go as a nurse and he to the front. Later, staying with the Brownlows, I found myself sitting in the formal garden at Belton surrounded with flowers, box bushes with tiny greenish flowers, quantities of narcissus, then lilac, while machine guns popped from the range near Belton Park. I had his letters from the front. How hard to learn that 'Le mieux est l'enemi du bien'.

We met in London too and danced at the Savoy. I was happy at these meetings, I know, though my clothes were not smart. And then he went back to the front. He wrote me letters describing lying in the sun at a gunpost, or getting into new billets. My attempt at nursing ended in influenza, and as the hospital authorities felt I was not born to the job, I came away, with a book full of portrait studies of tommies. So that spring found me with the Brownlows at Belton, with its wonderful beauty and its hospitality, formal and elegant, in house and garden. Half a mile away was a huge camp of soldiers. 'Dear fellows' Cousin Adelaide Brownlow called them. My cousin Louise Talbot and I helped to entertain them in the house. We sang good songs at Belton concerts – 'Little Grey Home in the West', 'The Broken Doll', 'A Little Bit of Heaven'. I sang all these and generally found a good accompanist on the spot, and of course Louise and I made friends with the bass and tenor in doing part-songs. It was all singing and all laughing, duets and walks round the garden, camp concerts at night.

All that spring young men were going to death, to an unknown fate; my Scottish friend who was killed, handsome young Canadians, little Englishmen and big, the good-looking artist I knew at Slade. Though overshadowed with threats it was a rich time of youth and ardour, with the beautiful house, the exquisite spring garden for background. Age embodied in handsome Adelaide Brownlow and her husband was delightful and gracious; their sympathy and life-long feeling for others went out to these officers and men so soon to go to the field of battle. On foggy cold spring nights, when the drafts of soldiers started from Grantham, we used to serve them with hot soup there, in the street outside the railway station. It was dark and grey, the soldiers stamped their feet on the hard road; they drank their soup, and then marched into the station yard and entrained. Next day would begin again with a lovely spring morning in the garden at Belton.

My portrait of my Brownlow cousins in the boat dated from that time; I greatly enjoyed doing it. Adelaide Brownlow died the following March, so I had made a little record of them together. I wept bitterly at the funeral service; even Mother thought my tears excessive. Cousin Adelaide seemed so bound up with my life, so noble, so kind, so irreplaceable. The past which I have been trying to evoke died with her.

My mother's death? – years later, when other interests and activities had claimed me – reawakened the gentle pain of nostalgia.

Like the little spring at Withington Rectory bubbling up in the grass and the water flowing on, so my life, sprung from these three Rectories, had flowed into other and irreconcilable channels. But Withington and its old Talbots and Elweses stayed in my mind; Kennington interested me; and Little Gaddesden, my earliest home, bound up with recollections of Ashridge, has been familiar all my life as a real place.

I am finishing this, in the Second World War, away from all three, but here too I can hear in the stillness at night a trickle of water, a spring. But, listen, there is a trinity of sound: the war planes rush overhead, and in a tree nearby sings the nightingale.

FINIS

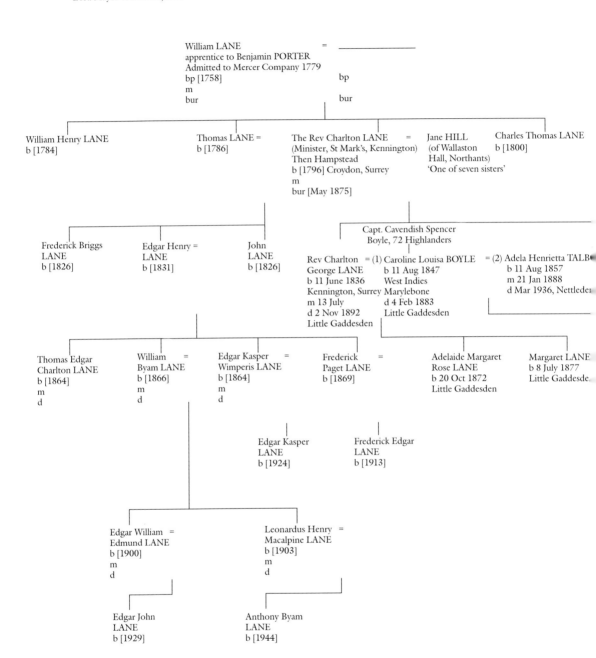

LANE   Pollock
Lord Mayor of London, 1697

William LANE   =   _____
apprentice to Benjamin PORTER
Admitted to Mercer Company 1779
bp [1758]   bp
m
bur   bur

William Henry LANE   Thomas LANE =   The Rev Charlton LANE   =   Jane HILL   Charles Thomas LANE
b [1784]   b [1786]   (Minister, St Mark's, Kennington) (of Wallaston   b [1800]
                                               Then Hampstead   Hall, Northants)
                                               b [1796] Croydon, Surrey   'One of seven sisters'
                                               m
                                               bur [May 1875]

Frederick Briggs   Edgar Henry =   John   Capt. Cavendish Spencer
LANE   LANE   LANE   Boyle, 72 Highlanders
b [1826]   b [1831]   b [1826]
                                              Rev Charlton   = (1) Caroline Louisa BOYLE   = (2) Adela Henrietta TALB●
                                              George LANE   b 11 Aug 1847   b 11 Aug 1857
                                              b 11 June 1836   West Indies   m 21 Jan 1888
                                              Kennington, Surrey Marylebone   d Mar 1936, Nettlede●
                                              m 13 July   d 4 Feb 1883
                                              d 2 Nov 1892   Little Gaddesden
                                              Little Gaddesden

Thomas Edgar   William   =   Edgar Kasper   =   Frederick   =   Adelaide Margaret   Margaret LANE
Charlton LANE   Byam LANE   Wimperis LANE   Paget LANE   Rose LANE   b 8 July 1877
b [1864]   b [1866]   b [1864]   b [1869]   b 20 Oct 1872   Little Gaddesde●
m   m   m   Little Gaddesden
d   d   d

                                 Edgar Kasper   Frederick Edgar
                                 LANE   LANE
                                 b [1924]   b [1913]

Edgar William =   Leonardus Henry =
Edmund LANE   Macalpine LANE
b [1900]   b [1903]
m   m
d   d

Edgar John   Anthony Byam
LANE   LANE
b [1929]   b [1944]

LANE TREE

MERCERS' COMPANY RECORDS ASSUMING ADMISSION AT AGE 21
CONSTANCE LANE'S BOOK
LITTLE GADDESDEN RECORDS
BAPTISMS - ST MARK'S, KENNINGTON
WESTMINSTER SCHOOL RECORDS

[ ] POSSIBLY

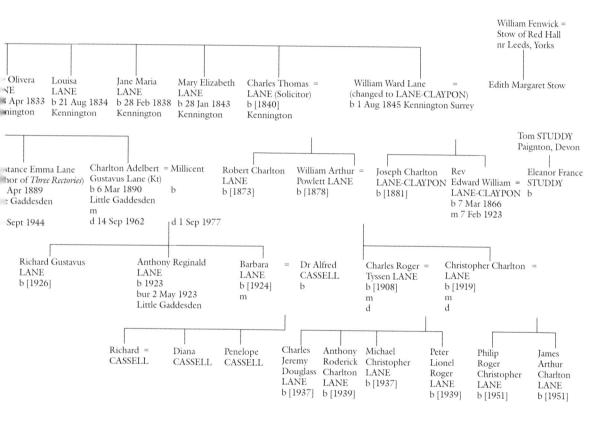

William Fenwick =
Stow of Red Hall
nr Leeds, Yorks

Olivera
NE
Apr 1833
nington

Louisa
LANE
b 21 Aug 1834
Kennington

Jane Maria
LANE
b 28 Feb 1838
Kennington

Mary Elizabeth
LANE
b 28 Jan 1843
Kennington

Charles Thomas =
LANE (Solicitor)
b [1840]
Kennington

William Ward Lane =
(changed to LANE-CLAYPON)
b 1 Aug 1845 Kennington Surrey

Edith Margaret Stow

Tom STUDDY
Paignton, Devon

stance Emma Lane
hor of *Three Rectories*)
Apr 1889
: Gaddesden

Sept 1944

Charlton Adelbert = Millicent
Gustavus Lane (Kt)
b 6 Mar 1890
Little Gaddesden
m
d 14 Sep 1962

b

d 1 Sep 1977

Robert Charlton
LANE
b [1873]

William Arthur =
Powlett LANE
b [1878]

Joseph Charlton
LANE-CLAYPON
b [1881]

Rev
Edward William =
LANE-CLAYPON
b 7 Mar 1866
m 7 Feb 1923

Eleanor France
STUDDY
b

Richard Gustavus
LANE
b [1926]

Anthony Reginald
LANE
b 1923
bur 2 May 1923
Little Gaddesden

Barbara =
LANE
b [1924]
m

Dr Alfred
CASSELL
b

Charles Roger =
Tyssen LANE
b [1908]
m
d

Christopher Charlton =
LANE
b [1919]
m
d

Richard =
CASSELL

Diana
CASSELL

Penelope
CASSELL

Charles
Jeremy
Douglass
LANE
b [1937]

Anthony
Roderick
Charlton
LANE
b [1939]

Michael
Christopher
LANE
b [1937]

Peter
Lionel
Roger
LANE
b [1939]

Philip
Roger
Christopher
LANE
b [1951]

James
Arthur
Charlton
LANE
b [1951]

TALBOT TREE

Based on comments in *Three Rectories* by Constance Emma Lane

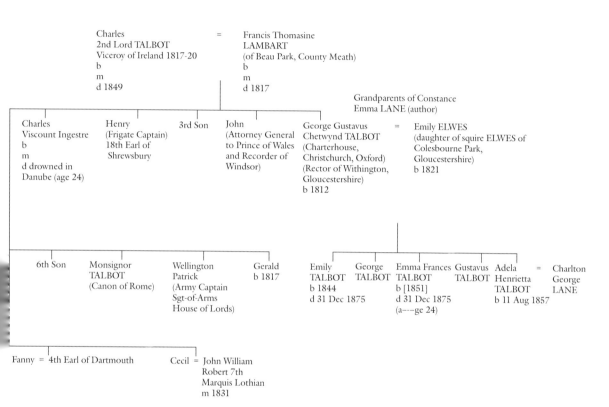

Charles
2nd Lord TALBOT
Viceroy of Ireland 1817-20
b
m
d 1849

=

Francis Thomasine
LAMBART
(of Beau Park, County Meath)
b
m
d 1817

Grandparents of Constance
Emma LANE (author)

Charles
Viscount Ingestre
b
m
d drowned in
Danube (age 24)

Henry
(Frigate Captain)
18th Earl of
Shrewsbury

3rd Son

John
(Attorney General
to Prince of Wales
and Recorder of
Windsor)

George Gustavus
Chetwynd TALBOT
(Charterhouse,
Christchurch, Oxford)
(Rector of Withington,
Gloucestershire)
b 1812

=

Emily ELWES
(daughter of squire ELWES of
Colesbourne Park,
Gloucestershire)
b 1821

6th Son

Monsignor
TALBOT
(Canon of Rome)

Wellington
Patrick
(Army Captain
Sgt-of-Arms
House of Lords)

Gerald
b 1817

Emily
TALBOT
b 1844
d 31 Dec 1875

George
TALBOT

Emma Frances
TALBOT
b [1851]
d 31 Dec 1875
(a---ge 24)

Gustavus
TALBOT

Adela
Henrietta
TALBOT
b 11 Aug 1857

=

Charlton
George
LANE

Fanny = 4th Earl of Dartmouth

Cecil =

John William
Robert 7th
Marquis Lothian
m 1831